Increasing Enrollment of African-American Males in Advanced High School STEM Courses

Increasing Enrollment of African American Males in High School Advanced Math & Science Classes

An Action Research Study

by

David R. Macauley, Ed.D.

Author	David R. Macauley, Ed.D., Los Angeles, CA
Publisher	DBC Publishing, Virginia Beach / Richmond, VA
ISBN	ISBN-13: 978-0692841723 (DBC Publishing) ISBN-10: 0692841725
Cover Art	Design cover by Dawn D. Boyer, Ph.D. (2017©) Cover: iStock purchased & licensed photos (2016/2017©); Title Page: Public Domain, Courtesy, Pixabay.com (2016)

Author Contact: Contact the author with questions, comments, research questions, or study inquiries at: davidrmacauley@gmail.com

TABLE OF CONTENTS

LIST OF TABLES

INCREASING THE ENROLLMENT OF AFRICAN-AMERICAN MALES IN ADVANCED MATHEMATICS AND SCIENCE COURSES IN HIGH SCHOOL

By

David R. Macauley, Ed.D.

Ed.D., 2014, Capella University, California
M.A. Ed., 2004, California State University,
Dominguez Hills
B.Sc. (Honors), 1990, Fourah Bay College,
University of Sierra Leone

A Dissertation Submitted to the Faculty of Capella
University in Partial Fulfillment of the Requirements
for the Degree of

DOCTOR OF EDUCATION

Capella University
September 2014
Copyright[(c)] 2014

Yvonne Barnes, Ed.D., Faculty Mentor / Chair
Alice Ledford, Ph.D., Committee Member
Michael Sanders, Ph.D., Committee Member
Feranda Williamson, Ed.D., Dean, School of Education

ABSTRACT

Increasing Enrollment of African-American Males in Advanced High School STEM Courses

This research study explored strategies to increase the enrollment of African-American male high school students in advanced mathematics and science courses at a public high school. A mentoring program was implemented that guided the student(s) for a period of 20 hours. The participants for the study included 15 African-American male students and 20 teachers, 10 of whom played the role of mentors and another 10 that took part in a survey. Participants for the study were purposefully chosen. Inclusion criteria were that all students were African Americans by ethnicity, had a grade of C or better in mathematics, and scored at the proficient or basic level in their most recent state standardized test in mathematics.

Surveys were documented and analyzed using the web-based commercial software Survey Monkey. Responses to interview questions were documented by hand.

Scholars have recommended novel and culturally responsive intervention programs to close the achievement gap of African-American high school males and their counterparts. The structured mentoring program builds on the ideals of social interaction with teachers playing the role of mentors.

The findings indicated when a mentoring program is structured and utilizes strategies, such as interacting with teachers beyond the classroom, discussing related careers in science and mathematics, and helping mentees develop good study habits, mentees reported an increased likelihood the students will enroll in advanced mathematics and science courses. More empirical studies on structured mentoring programs with African-American male high school students holds promise as an effective intervention to close the achievement gap in the mathematics and science pipeline.

ACKNOWLEDGEMENTS & DEDICATION

To my queen and bride, Molley, your faithful love, encouragement, and support lifts my spirit every morning, I am so blessed to have you on our life's journey. Nayo and Sholade, you inspire me every day to a better human being. To my late father and Mother, Magnus and Euphemia Macauley, and to the women who blazed many trails for me to walk through and whose handprints shaped and continue to impact my life: my 94-year-old aunt, my confidant and friend Rosamond Jones, and my only sibling and constant encourager, Magna Cole. I thank you.

Many thanks go to my mentor, Dr. Yvonne Barnes, for her guidance throughout the various stages of this project and to my committee members Dr. Alice Ledford and Dr. Michael Sanders, for their consistent review and recommendations. Finally, my heartfelt thanks and appreciation to Capella University, particularly the School of Education for an amazing experience over the last four years.

David R. Macauley

CHAPTER I

INTRODUCTION TO THE PROBLEM

African-American males are under-represented in advanced mathematics and science courses. The National Center for Education Statistics (2005) for 1982-2004 provides data on trends in mathematics and science course taking by sub-groups. The data revealed in 2004, the percentages of Asians, Caucasians, Hispanics and Blacks completing calculus studies were respectively, as follows: 34%, 16%, 7%, and 5%. Palmer, Davis, Moore, and Hilton (2010) indicated in their study that African-American males, except for Hispanics, are disproportionately represented compared to other sub-groups in the award of bachelor's degrees awarded to U.S. males in science and engineering. The breakdown is as follows: African Americans 5.3-6.1%, Asians/Pacific Islanders 7.8-9.4%, Hispanics 5.2-6.1%, and Caucasians 74-66.9%.

The data supports the claim African Americans in general, and are under-represented in advanced mathematics and science courses. This statistical trend is consistent with low enrollment of African-American male high school students in advanced mathematics and science courses at the public school in which this study was conducted.

There is a need to close the achievement gap between the African-American sub-group and their Asian and Caucasian counterparts. According to a report by the U.S. Department of Education, cited by Anderson (2008), needs – including targeted course pathways, extra academic help and relationship building with teachers – have prompted many educators to resort to intervention strategies that lack empirical support, and for this reason the expected outcomes are not realized. The assertion by Anderson alludes to common interventions implemented in the majority of public schools, including assigning failing students to after-school tutoring programs and Saturday tutoring programs, with the expectation students' grades will improve, not only in mathematics and science, but in all other subject areas. Therefore, more empirical studies are needed to investigate the effectiveness of intervention strategies. Anderson further comments that, although there is a lack of empirical support for intervention strategies, there is an emergence of youth programs and mentoring. Although some researchers tested the effectiveness of these youth and mentoring programs at the elementary, middle, and college levels, more action research needs to be undertaken in the area of increasing the enrollment of African-American male students in advanced mathematics and science courses at the high school level.

Research studies exist in academics documenting factors responsible for the achievement gap of African-American male students, but few reports offer intervention strategies that could alleviate the problem. Mentoring is one avenue by which the situation can be remedied (Gordon, Iwamoto, Ward, Potts, & Boyd, 2009). Research in mentoring focuses on middle school and college students with not enough valid and reliable documentation of mentoring activities in high schools where teachers play the role of mentor.

For example, a study done by Gordon et al. (2009) was conducted with middle school-aged black males. In this study the Benjamin E. Mays Institute (BEMI) utilized the tenets of mentoring to overcome barriers to "academic underachievement among adolescent black males by building a model that is Afro-centric, uses pro-social modeling, and emphasizes cultural strengths and pride" (p. 1). Sciarra (2010) posited that school counselors should support student expectations to attend college with appropriate curricular decisions. This study aimed to evaluate strategies that foster increased enrollment of African-American male students in mathematics and science courses in high school. The study drew from multiple perspectives including students' and teachers' perceptions and the social mentor/mentee interaction with specific emphasis on bridging the advanced mathematics and science achievement gap between the African-American male sub-group and their Caucasian and Asian male counterparts.

Background, Context, and Theoretical Framework

This action research study was conducted in a public high school in southern California. The school serves a multi-ethnic population of about 2,700 students. Approximately 58% of the student population is Hispanics, 25% are African Americans, 12% are Caucasians, and 5% are other races (Western Association of Schools and Colleges [WASC], 2010). Within the last five years, the public high school has created pathways to provide career options for students including health academy, business, engineering, and visual/performing arts.

Socio-economic factors coupled with in-school factors adversely affect student achievement. Over 70% of the students receive free or reduced lunch indicating the majority of students come from low-income families. The school, despite being equipped with qualified professional teachers, is faced with many challenges, including low graduation rates compared to the other high schools in the district and comparatively low annual percentage index (API), an indicator that measures how well the school prepared its students to succeed academically upon completion of yearly state standardized tests. Other challenges include discipline problems, lower academic rigor compared to similar high schools with the same demographics in the district, inadequate amount of advanced placement courses, and low enrollment of African-American students in advanced mathematics and science courses. Hispanics, Asians, and Caucasians of both sexes have a higher enrollment in advanced placement (AP) courses than African-American males. As a consequence, this school did not attain its target mark for the API in the 2011-2012 school years.

The findings of an informal teachers' meeting at the research-centric school in California in September of 2011 discovered teachers and counselors are under the assumption the low enrollment of African-American students in advanced mathematics and science courses is due to the students' lack of interest in these subjects. Counselors and teachers do not see any value in how science and mathematics can affect male African-American students' future coupled with socio-economic factors, such as single-parent homes and placement in foster-care homes. Despite these assumptions by counselors, the impression is that counselors and administration (in general) need to be more aware of the disparity and explore better intervention strategies to encourage African-American males to enroll in academically rigorous mathematics and science related courses.

Findings by the Western Association of Schools and Colleges (WASC; 2010) concur on inadequate preparation of African-American students for advanced classes in public schools. As one of six associations responsible for accreditation of public schools, WASC denoted that while the school is a safe environment, teachers generally hold low expectations for students, which impacts student achievement. The report also stated parental involvement in school activities is low (WASC, 2010). These challenges are further amplified by the teachers' union, which may not support incurred overtime of the staff to help alleviate the problems. This research study serves to provide a mentoring intervention to encourage African-American males to enroll in more challenging mathematics and science courses prior to graduation. The intervention may be challenged in the future by established district policies, as well as union policies. The principal of the research site high school proposed a mentoring initiative for the 2009-2010 school year, and this intervention provided a model by which a structured mentoring program could be implemented.

Researchers made assertions about possible factors affecting the academic achievement of African-American males (Graves, 2010; Palmer et al., 2010; Young, 2009). According to Graves, parents' academic expectations of African-American males decrease as the students' progress through elementary school in comparison to African American female students. Societal stereotypes seldom present African-American males as accomplished scientists and mathematicians, which is also a contributing factor to the achievement gap (Young, 2009). Palmer et al. posited there is a lack of encouragement by teachers and counselors to assist African-American males in enrolling in college preparatory courses.

For structuring the intervention, the researcher also reviewed literature by the Quality Education for Minorities (QEM). The idea of a mentor-mentee relationship is supported by the initiators of QEM (2010). The authors posited the development of a mentoring program for minority males at a local high school is one of the better strategies to increase enrollment in STEM (science, technology, engineering, and mathematics) related disciplines in college (QEM, 2010).

Theoretical Framework

This action research study is based on organizational learning theories. According to Argyris and Schon (2009), for organizations to change, stakeholders must model important theories of action. Two theories of organizational learning form a part of the theoretical framework for this unique study. First, single-loop versus double-loop learning, which Argyris and Schon described as "instrumental learning that changes strategies of action or assumptions in ways that leave the values of a theory of action unchanged" (2009, p. 21). Double-loop learning refers to "learning that results to a change in the values of theory in use as well as in its strategies and assumptions" (Argyris & Schon, 2009, p. 21). The applicability of this theory to the research is justified in that when students fail to perform at the level the organization expects, the organization seeks to fix the problem by offering interventions such as after-school tutoring with the anticipation the action will improve the student's academic achievements. This action leaves the values of the organization's theory of action unchanged. These latter illustrations also explain the single feedback loop evident in single-loop learning.

This action research study serves to question assumptions thereby providing an opportunity for an organization to change the values of the organizational entities' theory of action. The research topic, which is evaluating strategies to increase the enrollment of African-American male students in advanced mathematics and science courses, will explore the effect of mentoring as a novel approach to intervention. Factors affecting the achievement gap include African-American students' attitudes towards mathematics and science, teacher perceptions about the academic achievement of African-American male students, and parental involvement (Graves, 2010; White, 2009; Young, 2009). The outcome of the mentoring intervention itself provides a secondary feedback to evaluate existing norms and values of the organization which ultimately changes the values of its theory of action.

The second theory incorporates systems thinking. Aronson (1996) posited, "Systems thinking works by expanding its view to account for larger numbers of interactions as an issue is being studied" (p. 1). This concept is applicable to this action research study because it focuses on studying one sub-group, which impacts the whole system. To be complacent about the plight of the low enrollment of

African-American males in advanced level mathematics and science courses is to continue to do this population a disservice. The research was designed in accordance with action science principles which incorporated a series of inquiry steps including designing and implementation of an action plan. Management principles, such as diagnosing a problem, planning to solve the problem, organizing activities to implement the plan, evaluating results, and applying corrective measures (Herr & Anderson, 2005). The purpose of the study was to effectively communicate to all participants, and to have clearly communicated the role each one will play during the study.

Statement of the Problem

African-American male students were found to have a low enrollment in advanced mathematics and science courses in a public high school compared to their male counterparts in other sub-groups at the same public high school in southern California. This finding was revealed during the fall of 2012 when the researcher collected data to compare the enrollment of various male subgroups in advanced mathematics and science courses. The data indicated that lower numbers of African-American males were enrolled in advanced mathematics and science courses compared to males of the other ethnic sub-groups including Asians, Hispanics, and Caucasians. African-American males made up approximately10%

of the population of all students, and school superintendents expected a reasonable parentage of African-American males (at least 5%) enrolled in advanced mathematics and science courses. Compared to the larger population of all students in the school, only about 0.03% of African-American males were enrolled in advanced mathematics and science courses. Based on these statistics, it was evident African-American males were significantly under-represented in advanced mathematics and science courses and were over-represented in general education courses.

Purpose of the Study

The purpose of this action research study was to implement a mentoring program to prepare African-American males in grades 9-10 to improve their academic skills in mathematics and science and to meet the requirements for enrollment into these courses during their junior and senior years of high school.

Research Questions

Central Research Question

Can a structured mentoring program increase enrollment of African-American males in advanced mathematics and science courses in high school?

Sub-Questions

1. What attitudes do African-American male high school students hold toward mathematics and science courses?
2. What are high school teachers' perceptions or expectations about the enrollment of African-American males in advanced mathematics and science courses?
3. What are the elements of a structured mentoring program suitable for high school teachers to assume the role of mentors?
4. What is the impact of a high school-based mentoring program on the academic outcome of African-American males?

Rationale, Relevance, and Significance of the Study

African-American males have unique needs such as: being affirmed, relationship building, and motivation, but the reality of these unique needs often go unnoticed by educators. The intervention of a mentoring program will improve the current practices by which the African-American high school male students are guided to improve their chances of exploring science and mathematics related disciplines. Although the principal of the research site high school proposed teachers should choose at least two mentees from their assigned students, the initiative has been met with minimal success. This may have been due to the instructional staff's lack of training on how to be mentors, as well as a lack of empirical guidance (U.S. Education as cited in Anderson 2008). This research study's intervention findings may be the first step toward a structured high school campus-mentoring program.

A mentoring program also produces consequences to the larger system of successfully making the desired change for improving the academic achievement of AA males. Successful intervention can be adapted, to promote closing of the mathematics and science achievement gap in African-American males' performance school-wide. Second, increased participation of African-American males in science and mathematics disciplines have implications for improving global competitiveness in science and mathematics related job industries (Palmer et al., 2010). If the research site high school does not become proactive, the school may likely maintain the status quo, thereby graduating African-American males lacking pre-requisites to enroll in science and mathematics academic disciplines in college. The global effect is dependency on foreign skilled labor in scientific fields.

This study is relevant to the researcher's specialization area of leadership and management in that leadership requires a systems approach that will consider facets of multiple groups of students with diverse needs. A practitioner's role is to be reflective and effect changes with the hope of impacting a much larger change in the system. The findings of the study were shared with the site administration, and have the potential to influence policies pertaining to strategies to increase enrollment of the African-American sub-group in rigorous mathematics and science courses. A mentoring program will be a viable avenue for transforming the school's academic culture. If this change effort is not made, the school's API may remain stagnant since African-American males contribute significantly to the results of state standardized tests. The numbers of African-American male students enrolled in advanced mathematics and science courses may remain at the current low enrollment level without intervention.

Nature of the Study

The researcher is a biology teacher whose role in this action research study was purely investigative. The purpose of this study was to improve the academic performance of African-American males in mathematics and science courses in their freshman and sophomore (ninth and 10th grade) years so they are prepared to enroll in advanced mathematics and science courses in their junior and senior years (11th and 12th grades). The plan of implementing an intervention of a mentor-mentee program had the potential to be adapted school-wide.

Definition of Terms

Culturally responsive. To be culturally responsive is the ability of teachers to work proactively and assertively to understand, respect, and meet the needs of students from cultural backgrounds different from their own (Ford & Kea, 2009).

Action Research Study. The design for this study was a collaborative action research – a type of qualitative research in which action is taken and reflected upon to improve practice (Herr & Anderson, 2005). Action research is cyclical in nature involving four basic steps: diagnosing, planning action, taking action, and evaluating action (Coughlan & Brannick, 2009).

Assumptions, Limitations, and Delimitations

African-American (AA) male students at a public high school were challenged in the area of enrollment in advanced level mathematics and science courses compared to their male counterparts of other ethnic groups within the same school. This ethno-centric deficit was assumed to be partially due to the school environment. Some administrators, teachers, and counselors are not doing enough to prepare African-American males to acquire the necessary skills to enable them to enroll in a (more) challenging mathematics and science curriculum.

Teachers and administrators did not fully understand the cultural needs of male African-American students (Ford & Kea, 2009, Orthner, Jones-Sanpei, & Williamson, 2004). This study attempted to address specific and unique sub-cultural needs, such as feelings supported, cultural sensitivity, and self-awareness by implementing a structured, school-wide mentoring program. This action research study explored other contributing factors, such as African-American males' attitudes towards mathematics and science courses, as well as academic, high-school teacher perceptions and expectations about the engagement of African-American males in advanced placement courses in mathematics and science.

This research study focused on an action research intervention of male African-American students at the research site – a public, high school only. The findings may not be generalizable to all African-American male students of similar ages and schools. The study was limited to African-American males and did not include black male students from other national or ethnic origins. Having examined the data very closely, the researcher determined African-American male high school students' enrollment in advanced mathematics and science courses presented a greater concern than the numbers of African-American females. The findings of this action research study were limited to a short period of intervention lasting no more than 60 days. Although the study subtly mentioned certain socio-cultural issues as contributing factors to the established research study problem, it did not extensively include in its analyses the interplay of variables such as racism, tracking, and socio-economic factors, which have been the focus of critical theorists in minority education.

Organization of the Remainder of the Study

Chapter Two presented the theoretical framework for the study and an analysis, synthesis, and critique of the relevant research and methodological literature related to the problem of low enrollment of African-American males in advanced mathematics and science courses in ninth and tenth grade at a selected research site high school. Chapter Three described the research methodology chosen to respond to the problem and answer the research questions. Upon completion of the data collection and analysis, Chapter Four included an analysis of the data. The completed study concludes with Chapter Five consisting of a summary of the findings, the conclusions drawn from the data presented in Chapter Four, the implications for practice, and the relationships of the findings to the literature.

CHAPTER II

REVIEW OF LITERATURE

Introduction to the Literature Review

The underrepresentation of male African-American students in advanced mathematics and science courses particularly in public high schools across the USA posed a concern for the students' preparedness to choose careers in the science, technology, engineering, and mathematics (STEM) pipeline. Male African-American students were as intellectually capable as their male counterparts of other ethnic sub-groups (White, 2009). Literature exists documenting the underachievement of African-American males, not only in mathematics and science, but also in reading. There seemed to be an abundance of statistical reports of over-representation of African-American males in special education, truancy, and lower graduation rates. According to Garrow and Kaggwa (2012), young African-American boys were not performing academically well in school compared to their Caucasian counterparts; the authors support the notion that the problem was not just in academics, but also identifiable in graduation, suspension, and truancy rates. This research study section covered a broad overview of general factors contributing to the achievement gap of African-American male high school students, not only in mathematics and science but also in other academic areas to garner a more comprehensive understanding of the research problem. The literature was reviewed for effective strategies schools and communities can use to help close the mathematics and science achievement gap.

Review of the Research
and Methodological Literature

Research Literature

The paucity of the enrollment of African-American male students in advanced mathematics and science courses may have a direct effect on the numbers of African-American males pursuing careers in science, technology, engineering, and mathematics arenas. According to a report by Washington (2011), in the United States there was a decline in individuals pursuing careers as engineers, scientists, and mathematicians in all ethnic groups, but particularly in African Americans. Washington further documented that in 2009 African Americans received 1% of the degrees issued in science technologies and 4% of the degrees issued in mathematics and statistics, with less than 2% awarded a Ph.D. in the physical sciences. Considering the U.S. Census Bureau's 2008 extrapolation that the number of minorities was predicted to increase by the year 2050, making up 50% of the United States' population, it was of vital importance that empirical studies be conducted to enhance the success of under-represented racial and ethnic minorities in science, technology, engineering, and mathematics. A continuation of this trend may negatively impact economic growth for the United States as well as its global competitiveness.

Three key factors identified in the literature that had contributed to the academic achievement gap between African-American males and their counterparts of other ethnic sub-groups in other academic areas (noted below), not just in science and mathematics. This section present factors that generally affected African-American students in general education courses before presenting more specific academic literature on interest level, difficulty, and worthwhileness as factors of science and mathematics contributing to the mathematics and science achievement gap of African-American male high school students. This section also presented various interventions including mentoring offered as solutions to narrow the achievement gap.

The literature documents factors affecting the general academic achievement of African American students. Three key factors were discussed. The first factor described the notion of how students identify with academics. Many scholars assumed students' identification with academics was an important aspect of their success (Griffin, 2002; Osborne,

1999). Academic identification is operationally defined as "the extent to which academic pursuits and outcomes form the basis for global self-evaluation" (Osborne, 1999, p. 59). Osborne made the assertion that those students with a high identification (i.e. higher grades- scoring at or above the 80th percentile in state standardized tests, lower absenteeism- i.e. less than 10 days in a school year, and less than three behavior referrals in a school year) with academics were more apt to make progress academically since there was a relationship between their self-esteem and academic success.

Alternatively, if a student had low identification with academics, they were more likely to remove themselves from academic tasks resulting in poor academic performance. African-American students' school identification had a positive effect on the students' academic performance and success (Griffin, 2002; Griffin & Allen, 2006; Osborne, 1999). Similarly, research shows African-American males who planned to attend college were significantly more likely to perform better in school (Toldson, 2008). African-American males who verbalized their intention to attend a 4-year college demonstrated a commitment to this goal by enrolling in challenging courses, which enabled them to meet requirements for the 4-year college.

The constructs of identity and self-esteem as determinants of poor academic performance of African-American males are documented by scholars (Barton, 2003; Graham, Taylor, & Hurdley, 1998;

Ogbu, 1994; Poliakoff, 2006; Toldson, 2008).

Students' attitudes impact achievement. The findings of a study conducted by Bell (2010) stated the majority of African-American male students did not possess the social skills necessary for them to be successful in the classroom. The author refers to behaviors including raising hands, being called on, and following directions as social skills (Bell, 2010).

Student's negative attitudes towards school originated from an oppositional bias culture ideology (White, 2009). According to Fordham and Ogbu (1986), oppositional culture resulted from historical discriminatory acts by a dominant culture, which as a consequence, creates minimal educational opportunities for African-American students. African-American students may have been victims of stereotypical threats, which occurred when the targeted group exhibited and fulfilled the negative stereotype prophesied about them (Steele, 2003). Although these assertions gave insights into the psychological and social determinants of the achievement gap, much should be done to gain a better understanding of the roadblocks preventing African-American males from fully engaging and identifying with their school's curriculum. African-American male students should themselves bear some responsibility for their own learning, and they must find creative ways to mitigate the challenges derailing their academic success.

A second factor contributing to the achievement gap between African-American males and their counterparts of other ethnic sub-groups is socio-economics (SES), particularly household income and nutrition (White, 2009). According to White, one socio-economic factor frequently associated with the achievement gap is poverty. The author stated that by the time a student entered kindergarten and first grade, mathematics and reading achievement gaps between poor students and their more socio-economically affluent counterparts are already present. The reason was that students from lower, socio-economic backgrounds did not have reading materials and were therefore not exposed to language development within the home. Other scholars also documented poverty as a barrier to the academic achievement of African-American males. According to Toldson (2008), African-American males coming from affluent homes have a greater chance of performing better. Although SES factors tended to inhibit the academic growth of students, more research is required to determine how the academic needs of low-income minority students could be met.

There was a correlation between SES factors and schools the low-income students could have attended. Battey (2013) argued students from low socio-economic backgrounds in urban areas tend to attend schools where teacher quality, in terms of qualification and knowledge of the subject matter, is less than satisfactory. Moreover, Museus, Palmer,

Davis, and Maramba (2011) documented that Blacks, Latinos, and other low SES minority students are at a disadvantage as a result of disparities in school funding. The report-documented students in communities where the residents pay less taxes, receive less funding than their affluent counterparts. Disparity affects availability of resources, which impacts the educational outcome of the under-served students. For example, in some high minority (70% of the students are Latinos, Asians, or other non-white ethnic group) public schools were either not equipped with science laboratories or had inadequate science laboratories, thus were unable to support the growing population of students. Lack of scientific resources may have resulted in negative outcomes on the science achievements of African-American students in poorly funded schools.

Although poverty was a contributing factor to the achievement gap of African-American students and other minorities in research identified by the literature review, it cannot be accepted as a panacea for low academic outcomes. According to Maydun (2011), proper social ties in the community could serve as a conduit to overcome the negative consequences associated with poverty. The author argued if social ties were developed within the community, despite the poverty that exited in the neighborhood, there was a greater chance the community (as a whole) would have developed norms that impacted positive academic outcomes for its youth (Maydun, 2011). One could concur with

Maydun's argument in that some African-American students reared in poor homes still emerged to be academically successful; a premise that confirmed that poverty in itself is not a reason for poor academic performance in school.

The report by White (2009) also documented that nutrition affected achievement. White referenced a study by the Congressional Black Caucus Foundation, which stressed the importance of utilizing nutritious food, such as vegetables into diets along with the academic experiences of African-American males. This assertion aligned with the view of several authorities in the health profession who contended that vegetables were necessary for proper brain function. In an article titled "Breaking Barriers," Toldson (2008) supported the assertion that eating raw vegetables was associated with higher levels of academic achievement. Although the focus of this action research study is on mentoring African-American males so they can enroll in challenging science and mathematics courses, the need to understand the interplay of factors such as nutrition and its effect on student achievement contributed to a thorough understanding of the research studies' problem.

A third factor contributing to the achievement gap of African-American students and other minorities is teacher expectations and perceptions. According to White (2009), teacher attitudes and expectations can impact student achievement. White commented a phenomenon known as 'stereotype threat' influences the way teachers viewed students and the way students viewed themselves. The phenomenon of stereotype threat explained why teachers had low achievement expectations of the minority students; the teachers' lower expectation of the students is based on the current performance of the students rather than the students' potential to perform (Kober, 2001). On issues pertaining to perceptions of school, relationships with teachers are also documented. Toldson (2008) asserted negative perceptions of school and hostile teacher-student relationships could negatively impact the academic achievement of African-American male students.

Although literature documented factors that contributed to the achievement gap of African-American males compared to their counterparts of other ethnic groups, there were scanty reports or a lack of empirical studies that specifically attempted to understand the causes of low enrollment of African-American males in science and mathematics. One study by Jenkins (1976) in the late 70s at Palatka High School in Florida explored black students' attitude towards taking science by way of administering an attitudinal survey. The variables explored were interest, difficulty, worthwhileness, and aptitude. The results indicated various responses depending on how the question was framed. Students who indicated they did not plan to take any additional science classes stated science was boring, challenging, and that reading science was difficult. The converse was true for students who indicated a preference for enrolling in advanced science courses. Although the study did not suggest any intervention for the black students who had negative perceptions about science, the premise provided insight into successful instructional strategies that could motivate students to enroll in advanced science courses, including evaluation of strategies to increase the enrollment of African-American males in science and mathematics. A similar attitudinal survey was designed in which students' responses were analyzed for perceptions about whether mathematics and science were challenging and/or boring. The results provided an understanding of how African-American males feel about these subjects and hence determined how mathematics and science teachers can be innovative in their instructional approach in teaching these subjects to students, particularly to those African-American male students who held negative views about science and mathematics.

African American students and Latino students were not prepared to undertake college level courses in mathematics according to Noble and Morton (2012). Two reasons attested to this claim: (a) the pattern of mathematics course taking, and (b) enrollment in advanced mathematics courses in previous years. This assertion supported the need for this unique action research study. For instance, students who have taken Algebra 1 prior to their ninth-grade year have a better chance of enrolling in advanced sections of mathematics before graduation. Further, Noble and Morton alluded to two factors that contributed to the low enrollment in advanced mathematics course. First, they argued lack of parent involvement in either directly helping the students with mathematics or failing to find a strong support system for them would negatively impact mathematics achievement. Second, student readiness for college plays a role. The authors posited students who have a goal to attend a 4-year college are more prepared for college level mathematics. This observed trend in a mathematics course-taking pathway was paramount to the action research. Techniques employed by mentors will be evaluated to determine effective instructional strategies that would and could motivate, as well as encourage African-American male high school students to enroll in advanced level mathematics and science courses prior to graduation.

Ethnic minority students are lagging behind their Caucasian counterparts in pursuing STEM-related courses in college. According to Museus et al. (2011), two key reasons prevent Blacks, Latinos, and Native Americans from preparing to enroll in science, technology, engineering, and mathematics related disciplines in college: (a) under-representation in advanced placement courses and (b) placement into remedial courses in high school. Prior to the planning of the study, a preliminary survey conducted at the research site revealed an under-representation of African-American males in advanced sections of mathematics and science courses and an over-representation in low-level mathematics and science courses compared to their male counterparts of other ethnic sub-groups. While statistics may be true generally, one must question the potential of complacency of minority parents to act in their children's best interest. Counselors scheduled students into specific courses based on the student's standardized test results. Parents and students themselves have a responsibility to track their own college pathway given the academic opportunities available.

Because of deficit reports on the progress of African-American males, academic scholars suggested promising interventions schools and communities could employ to alleviate some of the academic problems African-American males encounter in school. One avenue that offered a solution is raising black male achievement through school-based partnerships. According to Garrow and Kaggwa (2012), one such partnership is the Concerned Black Men (CBM) national organization. The CBM operation involves an initiative that produces positive academic and social outcomes for young black boys, including truancy reduction and raising academic performance. A key strategy pertinent to CBM partnerships is the implementation of a mentoring program to encourage male African-American high school students to enroll in advanced mathematics and science courses while still in high school.

There are reports of using mentoring to curb negative behaviors. Mentoring as a strategy to improve academic performance is paramount in this unique action research study. This finding was supported by Gordon et al. (2009), who conducted a study with urban middle school students in Hartford, Connecticut that showed sixth-grade students in the Benjamin E. Mays Institute (BEMI) mentoring program had a higher Grade Point Average (GPA) when compared to a comparison group of similar students (2.8 GPA versus 1.06 GPA). The BEMI group was found to identify more with academics than the comparison group.

Another study supported the construct of mentoring strategies to improve the academic performance of high school students. Black, Grenard, Sussman, and Rohrbach (2010) studied 3,320 high school students from 14 school districts in eight states (California, Arizona, Kansas, Louisiana, South Carolina, Washington, Maryland, and Massachusetts) and found students with naturally occurring mentoring relationships (e.g., successful adults who stand in the gap of missing or passive parents, and coach troubled youth to succeed in school and community) had a higher level of school attachment and hence improved academic and responsible behavior patterns. Black et al. mentioned how an analysis of the long-term impact of Sponsor-a Scholar program resulted in higher GPAs for students who followed the advice, encouragement, and instructions of their mentors. These studies indicate when students have extra support beyond the classroom, the results produced positive academic outcomes.

Mentoring as an intervention for the disadvantaged and at-risk youth produced positive outcomes. According to Tierney and Grossman (2000), adult men served as role models to disadvantaged youths including youth without fathers the result of which yielded positive outcomes. One such program that had national recognition is the Big Brothers/Big Sisters Program (BBBS). The assumption is adults can influence youth to develop healthy habits, which culminated in positive personal development of the youth. Unlike the BBBS program, this action research study focused on a mentoring program that targeted promising African-American male high school students whose teachers acted as mentors to motivate and developed their interests in science and mathematics. Although the BBBS program has value, it is suitable for at-risk and disadvantaged youths within a larger community context versus a smaller academically-focused setting in the classroom.

Studies prior to 2014 in the mentoring discourse of disadvantaged and minority youth that document culturally sensitive and detailed school-wide approaches were promising interventions that seem to work well for low-income and diverse students. One such approach was the Rites of Passage Program (ROP). The philosophical basis of the program was rooted in the resilience theory, which postulated individuals can succeed despite hardship (West-Olatunji, Shure, Garrett, Conwell, & Rivera, 2008). The outcome of resiliency, documented in a recent study, showed resilient, low-income families benefit from healthy family communication, economic resources, and a social network of support (Orthner, Jones-Sanpei, & Williamson, 2004). ROP programs instilled (in students) the connection between academic achievement and relevance to their community. The ROP program helped marginalized youth develop cultural and personal identity. Although rewarding, the focus of such a program was effective within the larger context of the community. However, educators could hone cultural practices of the ROP program as a necessary strategy to assist marginalized youth within the schools they attended. African-American males possessed resilient characteristics, such as coping skills, interpersonal relationships, and the acquisition of knowledge through feelings and emotion (West-Olatunjie et al., 2008).

Part of the goal of the mentoring intervention program is to provide an avenue for African-American male students to form relationships with teachers, thereby giving students the opportunity to express their thoughts about mathematics and science courses. Utilizing these strength-based attributes yielded promising results of teachers acting in the role of mentors. Embedded within the mentoring intervention program of this action research study were opportunities to build interpersonal relationships. The opportunity for mentees to interact with mentors on a more personal level, while acquiring knowledge and skills of mathematics and science, helped satisfy culturally sensitive attributes.

As noted, to close the achievement gap between African-American males and their counterparts of other ethnic groups, Anderson (2008) mentioned that intervention strategies were often prescribed offering promises unmet due to the lack of empirical evidence to substantiate claims of success. Reiterating Anderson's assertion more empirical support was needed, academic discourse has emerged in areas such as youth development and mentoring regarding how these interventions impact student achievement. These dialogues focus on curbing negative behavior among African-American males to attempt to produce positive outcomes for young black males. Key to this action research study was the implementation of a mentoring program to encourage African-American male students to enroll in advanced mathematics and science courses in high school. The few available research proposals relevant or pertaining to this action research study focus were only on academic improvements involving a wide range of general education courses. Little literature exists on strategies to increase the enrollment of African-American males in high school level advanced mathematics and science. One study, with similar goals of this action research study, was conducted by Jenkins (1976). Jenkins explored students' attitude towards taking science classes. The study explored variables such as interest, difficulty, worthwhileness, and aptitude. It is interesting to note this research was conducted over 30 years ago and provided a blueprint for strategies to increase the enrollment of black students in advanced mathematics and science. It had been given little attention by academic researchers of this discourse.

Review of Methodological Literature

There is a dearth of empirical studies on school-based structured mentoring that mirrored the purpose and research design implemented in this action research study. Three key research designs in the literature utilized methods that parallel the choice of the research design for this study. One study was the Benjamin E. Mays Institute (BEMI), a program conducted in Hartford, CT (Gordon et al., 2009) for mentoring urban middle school students. The methods employed for the BEMI program, although confined to middle school, were similar to the present action research study in the following areas: (a) procedures involved consent and approval by parents, students, and school to administer the surveys; (b) students' participation was optional, and they could withdraw at any time; and (c) criteria for participation were similar to selected students demonstrations of some degree of responsibility, such as cooperation, determination, and focus. The researcher for the current research study assumed students with a grade of C or better and scoring at the basic or proficient level in student standardized tests possessed the aforementioned attributes. The measures for the BEMI study were, however, different in that researchers used a quantitative methodology to analyze the data. The sample size of the student participants included a total of 61 students as opposed to 12 students for this unique action research study.

In another study, African-American male students' experiences of 'mattering to others' was investigated (Tucker, Dixon, & Griddine, 2010). Although not a mentoring program, the design validated some methods used in this action research study. For example, the study was conducted in a high school with face-to-face interviews using a sample size of nine African-American students. The criteria for participation included an academic grade of C and students must not have any records of disciplinary problems. The Tucker et al. research methodology was qualitative, and transcripts were analyzed for meanings from which discussions about the students' perceptions were generated.

A third study more aligned with the purpose of this action research study was an investigation of causes of low enrollment of black students in upper level math and science courses mentioned above (Jenkins, 1976). The study is different from this action research study in that there was no intervention planned, only documentation of causes.

Attitudinal surveys generated a discussion of students' perception of enrolling in upper level science courses. The instrument used for surveying the students was very similar to the one employed in this action research study.

Generally speaking, most of the published research on interventions that addressed the achievement gap of African-American males involved large samples of participants, were longitudinal in nature, and used quantitative methodology. For this action research study, the research design best suited was a qualitative action research. The reasons being: the study covered a short period, involved a small sample of students and teacher participants, 12 and 20 respectively. The input of teachers and students acting as mentors was vital to solving the problem statement explored in this research study. The design for this action research study was instrumental in not only generating knowledge, but included personal, professional, organizational, and community empowerment. This assertion is supported by Herr & Anderson, 2005. The research methodology enabled the researcher to collaborate with stakeholders in the organization and therefore provided the opportunity to reflect on the research process, as well as the findings.

Synthesis of the Research Findings

The research topic was, "Evaluating Strategies to Increase the Enrollment of African-American males in Advanced Mathematics and Science Courses." To fully understand the research problem, factors contributing to the achievement gap of African-American male high school students compared to their counterparts of other ethnic subgroups were identified in the literature. Ways to mitigate the causes of the achievement gap of African-American males in language arts, social studies, with mathematics and science in particular, were explored.

The literature documented an abundance of research pertaining to the underachievement of African-American males were not only in mathematics and science, but also in reading. Literature articles were published identifying suspension, truancy, and low graduation rates. Three factors are consistent throughout the literature as key causes of the achievement gap of African-American males: (a) students' low identification with academics, 1999), (b) students who identify with low academics tend to do poorly in academics , and (c) students who had a high identification with academics perform well academically(Griffin, 2002; Griffin & Allen, 2006; Osborne).

The literature documented a correlation between socio-economic factors and academic performance noting low-income students who lacked the necessary materials were apt to perform poorer academically than students generally from high income families (Toldson, 2008; White, 2009). The literature also documented the assertion of teacher expectations and perceptions of African-American males as a determinant of students' behavior and academic performance (Kober, 2001). Relevant to the causes of an identified low affiliation of African-American males in STEM careers, the literature was consistent in attributing the cause to a low enrollment of African-American males in advanced placement and college-preparatory classes while in high school, which was necessary to prepare the students to enroll in science, technology, engineering, and mathematics related disciplines in a 4-year college (Museus et al., 2011; Noble & Morton, 2012).

In the methodological literature, research designs that mirrored the design for the current study were minimal in documenting large sample sizes, longitudinal studies, and quantitative analyses of the data. The design for this study was participatory. The participatory aspect of this study is supported by Stringer (2007) who referred to the philosophical nature of academic research. Stringer compared participatory action research with other research paradigms and comments:

Unlike quantitative research (sometimes
referred to as experimental or positivistic
research) that is based on the precise definition,
measurement, and analysis of the relationship
between a carefully defined set of variables,
action research commences with a question,
problem, or issue that is rather broadly defined.
Investigations therefore seek initially to clarify
the issue investigated and to reveal the way
participants describe their actual experience of
that issue— how things happen and how it
affects them. (Stringer, 2007, p. 19)

Thus, the input, and strategies utilized by
students and teachers as stakeholders of the
organization aligned well with Stringer's participatory
action research paradigm. This claim, however, did
not discredit quantitative methods that could have
added value to the body of knowledge, but such
methods did not form the central core of the
investigative process in this study. To effectively
address the achievement gap regarding interventions,
a school-based structured mentoring approach
involving the participation of the teachers and
students was essential. The choice of the research
design required participatory action research that
promoted organizational learning (Stringer, 2007).

Critique of Previous Research

Although the literature documented intervention strategies that would help close the achievement gap in the academic performance of African-American males, most of the studies and proposed interventions generally focused on improving general academic performance and social behaviors, such as violence prevention and suspension and truancy reduction. Very little documentation existed that addressed specific interventions that maximized the potential of academically promising African-American males to enroll in challenging courses in science and mathematics while in high school. The identified literature review studies were deficit in that they focused on portraying African-American males as being culturally deprived and destined to be victims of the educational system.

Scholars, who assert there is evidence of psychological and social factors affecting the achievement of African-American males, provided useful insights into understanding the causes. Osborne (1999) discussed the relationship between self-esteem and academic success stating that low identification with academics was a precursor to low academic performance and vice versa. While this assertion held value, Osborne did not offer solutions to improve the self-esteem of students who failed to identify with academics.

Added to these deficit reports was the documentation of poverty as a barrier to academic achievement of African-American male students, most of whom were from low-income families. Although poverty was a contributing factor, it was not an excuse for low academic performance. For instance, Maydun (2011) posited that proper social ties in the community could lessen the impact of poverty but could also lead to development of norms that yielded positive outcomes. Documentation of course-taking pathways, such as the over-representation of African-American males in remedial science and mathematics courses and an under-representation in advanced placement science and mathematics courses (Museus et al., 2011; Noble & Morton, 2012) were stated without suggesting essential strategies that could have helped counselors and teachers. According to White (2009), schools should make available rigorous course work via advanced placement and honors courses.

Summary

The review of the literature highlighted how individual factors (poverty, identification with academics, self-esteem, nutrition, and identity), parental factors, and in-school factors (teacher expectations, lack of culturally responsive instruction, and limited funding) provided insight into a comprehensive understanding of the root causes of the African-American male achievement gap. The literature highlighted strategies such as mentoring, high identification with academics, and culturally sensitive instruction as strategies to close the achievement gap. Despite these useful interventions, no published research had fully deciphered how these factors collectively interacted and contributed to the success of African-American male high school students. There was a paucity of published research of interventions and research designs that employed participatory action research. There was a lack of empirical studies with specific emphasis on mentoring African-American male high school students so the students were better prepared to take on challenging courses in mathematics and science.

CHAPTER III

METHODS AND PROCEDURES

Introduction

In this chapter, a detailed methodology for the study was discussed. The discussion entailed the research design, including target population, sample size, setting, and recruitment. Further, a discussion on instrumentation, data collection method, field test, data analysis procedures, limitations of the research design, credibility, transferability, expected findings, and ethical issues was presented.

Purpose of the Study

The purpose of this study was to improve the academic performance of African-American males in mathematics and science courses in their freshman and sophomore (ninth and tenth grades) years so they were encouraged to enroll in advanced mathematics and science courses in their junior and senior years (11th and 12th grades). In this regard, the plan of implementing an intervention of a mentor-mentee program had the potential for adaptation school-wide. Although there were some interventions to help failing students such as the CBM and BBBS programs, these programs were neither gender nor ethnic specific. A structured mentoring intervention that addressed the science and mathematics gap achievement gap in African American high school students compared to their male counterparts was needed.

Research Questions and Hypotheses

Central Research Question

Can a structured mentoring program increase enrollment of African-American males in advanced mathematics and science courses in high school?

Sub-Questions

1. What attitudes do African-American male high school students hold toward mathematics and science courses?
2. What are high school teachers' perceptions or expectations about the enrollment of African-American males in advanced mathematics and science courses?
3. What are the elements of a structured mentoring program suitable for high school teachers to assume the role of mentors?
4. What is the impact of a high school-based mentoring program on the academic outcome of African-American males?

Research Design

The goal of the study was to evaluate the effects of strategies to increase the enrollment of African-American males in advanced mathematics and science courses at a public high school. One way to achieve this goal was to implement an intervention program where teachers of African-American male students would act as mentors over a specified period of time (i.e., 20 hours for this unique action research study). Study participants (i.e., students and their teachers) were to work collaboratively with the researcher to attain the goal of the study. The nature of the study involved an intervention and thus required a design that elicited action. The central research question for the study was, "Can a structured mentoring program increase enrollment of African-American males in advanced mathematics and science courses in high school?"

To find answers to the central research question collaborative efforts of key stakeholders in the organization (i.e., students and their teachers) was required. An action research design was best suited for the study. Herr and Anderson (2005) supported this assertion and commented that action research methodology was ideal in collaboration with those who have a stake in the issue investigated. Herr and Anderson explained the cyclical nature of action research, which involves developing a plan of action to improve the status quo, to act on the plan, to implement the plan, to observe the results of action within the environment in which it is happening, and finally to reflect on the results as a foundation for future planning. This action research study entailed only the first phase of the cycle; however, the study had potential for continued planning and action.

Action research is also based on Stringer's (2007) participatory action research paradigm. Stringer commented that participatory action research should include all stakeholders in the entire research process including the planning, methodology, implementation, and discussion of the results. Although the study involved a collaborative stance with teachers, students, and researcher it was not entirely participatory as described by Stringer. Teachers partially contributed to the methodology when they supplied input via a list of strategies they used in working with their mentees.

According to Reason and Bradbury (as quoted in Coughlan & Brannick, 2009), "Action research is defined as a participatory, democratic process concerned with developing practical knowing in the pursuit of worthwhile human purposes grounded in a participatory worldview" (p. 1). This democratic process of action research was further explained by those who posited different purposes for action research with two of the purposes being personal and political. For a personal purpose, Gall, Gall, and Borg (2009) stated one outcome of action research was to create a high degree of concern in practitioners. For example, practitioners can clearly examine their assumptions about education and call into question contradictions between their espoused theory and actual classroom practices. For a political purpose, Gall et al. asserted action research embraced an overt agenda of social change with the result of promoting social justice through collaborative efforts that leads to increased educational opportunities and outcomes for all stakeholders. Such efforts, according to Gall et al., addressed issues of sex, class, cultural equity, and voice in education. Keeping these intentions of action research in mind, the nature of the study justified a research design that elicits action. The ultimate goal of increasing the enrollment of promising African-American males in advanced mathematics and science required a democratic process involving the participation of both students and their teachers whose experiences are revealed during interviews and surveys conducted by the researcher.

Target Sample, Sampling Method, and Related Procedures

Target Population and Sample

The target population were all African-American males in the ninth and tenth grades at the research site high school. The sample for the study consisted of 12 African-American male students in ninth and tenth grade with ages ranging from 14 to

16 with a grade of at least a C in their current mathematics courses at the time of the study. In addition, they must have scored at the basic or proficient level in mathematics in their most recent standardized test score.

Sampling Method

The sampling method was convenience and purposive sampling (Gall et al., 2009). The convenience method was chosen over other methods because the researcher sought to change the status quo in regards to issues affecting the targeted population (all ninth and tenth grade African-American males). The method was also purposive in that student participants within the organizational context were representative of the issue investigated were sufficient match of sample population to overall population. For example, a finding of a preliminary investigation by the researcher denoted African-American males are under-represented in advanced mathematics and science courses compared to their counterparts of other ethnic groups. Therefore, convenience and purposive methods were the best fit for the action research study.

Sample Size

The sample consisted of 12 African-American male students, 10 teachers who served as mentors, and another 10 teachers that participated in an online survey (only). The participating African-American male students met the criteria for participation and remained committed throughout the mentoring intervention. In addition, the 12 students were typically representative of potentially promising African-American male students at the research site. Critical to this intervention was the commitment by the mentor and mentee to meet outside of regular school hours to achieve any meaningful interaction.

Setting

The action research took place in a public high school located in southern California. Participants met in their classrooms either before school, during lunch, and or after school. The researcher met with teacher participants during their conference periods and after school to conduct face-to-face interviews. The researcher also met with student participants at the guidance-counseling center to conduct the research-centric interviews.

Recruitment

Recruitment of participants took place by disseminating three letters to three groups of stakeholders at the research site. A recruitment letter for students was sent to the counselors (Appendix B). The counselors were asked to compile a list of eligible students per the stated inclusion criteria for participation. Several counselors responded, after which a list of eligible African-American male students was complied. The researcher then met with the eligible students in the guidance office and hand-delivered a recruitment letter to them during the meeting. In recruiting teachers to serve as mentors, the researcher sent out blanket copy e-mails to all teachers (Appendix C). All recruitment letters clearly stated the purpose and expectation of the intended action research.

A total of 15 students responded and desired to participate; however, only 12 of the 15 students met all the inclusion criteria for participation. The students were each given two letters of informed consent: one for their parents and one for themselves (Appendix D and E). Students who brought back signed letters of consent were accepted to participate. The researcher invited all student participants to an informational meeting prior to the implementation of the study. Furthermore, 20 teachers gave consent to participate. Ten of the teachers participated only in an online survey and another 10 teachers served as mentors, as well as participated in the online survey.

Instrumentation

Although the research design was qualitative, two surveys were designed in order to garner a variety of responses from participants. All surveys were, however, analyzed qualitatively. The surveys were reviewed and evaluated by three content experts. All revisions offered by the panel of experts were addressed. Suggestions deemed to improve the readability, comprehension, objective, and overall presentation of the surveys were incorporated into the final copy. Lastly, two sets of interviews were conducted: one with the mentors and the other with the mentees using five semi-structured interview questions also reviewed by the panel of experts. Per the suggestions of the experts, the questions reflected objectivity, probing questions, and allowed for clarification of any issues needing further exploration.

Field Test

Three experts reviewed the researcher created instruments including the survey questions and the interview questions. All three experts offered feedback regarding the appropriateness of the survey and interview questions. Field tests were conducted prior to Institutional Review Board (IRB) approval. On the original survey instrument the following suggestions were provided by the expert reviewers: a 1-5 point Likert-type scale rather than a descriptive scale was preferred because a 1-5 point Likert-type scale gives greater facility to analyze data (i.e., computation of average ratings in the surveys was instrumental in the analyses), some questions required options so respondents had a range of choices, use of consistent language throughout the instrument, avoidance of using questions that may require empirical evidence, and inclusion of questions pertaining to mentoring. For comments regarding the interview questions, one expert reviewer suggested interview questions should be framed in such a way that respondents could articulate a wide variety of responses. For example, it would be better to ask respondents about the benefits they obtained from the intervention rather than ask them about the success of the intervention. Suggestions deemed to improve the credibility, readability, understanding, and purpose of the surveys were incorporated into the final products.

Data Analysis Procedures

This section described how the data analysis plan of action provides data directly responsive to the research questions. All data sets were analyzed using emergent theme analysis and an inductive process where the data were coded were coded into broad categories, ultimately, inductive reasoning was used to help answer broadly stated questions. The methodology employed thick description and triangulation of data. The central research question was, "Can a structured mentoring program increase enrollment of African American males in advanced mathematics and science courses in high school?" To answer the central question sub-questions were framed to articulate a wide variety of responses.

Data Collection

The research design was qualitative. The first survey solicited teacher perceptions about African American male students' attitudes towards mathematics and science, and the second survey was on students' attitudes towards mathematics and science. Both surveys consisted of 10 statements with responses using 1-5 Likert-type rating scale with a write-in response option. According to McMillan (2011), a Likert-type scale was useful for measuring levels of agreement where "subjects indicate their attitudes or values by checking the place on the scale that best reflects their feelings and beliefs about the statement." Numbers were used on a scale of 1-5, with a '1' denoting that participant *strongly disagrees* with the statement, a '3' indicating that the participant *somewhat agrees,* and a '5' denoting that participant *strongly agrees* with the statement. The choice of a Likert-type scale aligned with the researcher's goal of understanding preferences since these preferences influenced motivation, which in turn may have influenced student achievement (McMillan 2011).

The researcher posted both surveys online through SurveyMonkey.com for easy participant access. Four instruments were used to collect data: (a) survey with students, (b) survey with teachers, (c) interviews, and (d) progress report.

Survey on students' attitudes towards mathematics and science. This data consisted of 10 statements using a 1-5 Likert-type scale. Students took the survey online during the implementation phase of the action research. The purpose of this instrument was to determine perceptions that students hold regarding mathematics and science. The data provided insight to the researcher for understanding how a mentoring program could best be structured. Jenkins (1976) used a similar attitudinal survey to understand factors affecting the low enrollment of African-American students in upper level science courses at Palatka high school.

Survey on teacher perceptions. This survey consisted of 10 statements with responses using a 1-5 Likert-type scale with an option for a written response. Twenty teachers took the survey online. Teacher perceptions are important determinants of utilizing teachers to serve as mentors. An evaluation of teachers' various perceptions informed elements of a structured program for them to assume the role of mentors. For example, teacher perceptions regarding the attitudes of African-American males in academics, mathematics and science in particular, might provide useful information that could and/or should be considered when training teachers prior to their induction as mentors to encourage potentially promising African-American male students to enroll in advanced mathematics and science courses.

Interviews. Two sets of interviews were conducted after the conclusion of the mentoring intervention part of the study: one with the mentors and one with the mentees. The purpose of the interviews was to evaluate the effects of strategies to increase the enrollment of African-American males in advanced mathematics and science courses. The interviews consisted of five questions. The researcher scheduled interviews with mentors and mentees within one week and documented all responses.

Progress report. The researcher, in collaboration with the mentors, designed a biweekly progress report used to monitor the progress of the mentoring intervention. Each mentor provided feedback biweekly indicating what strategies they used with their mentees every two weeks (see Appendix). The biweekly report was highly instrumental in monitoring progress of the intervention(s).

Data Analysis Procedures

This section described how the data analysis plan of action provides data directly responsive to the research questions. All data sets were analyzed using emergent theme analysis and an inductive process where the data were coded into broad categories. Ultimately, inductive reasoning was used to help answer broadly stated questions. Also, the methodology employed thick description and triangulation of data. The central research question was, "Can a structured mentoring program increase enrollment of African-American males in advanced mathematics and science courses in high school?" In order to answer the central question, sub-questions were framed to articulate a wide variety of responses.

Sub-Question 1

What attitudes do African-American male students hold toward mathematics and science courses?

To answer this question, participating students took an online survey. The survey consisted of 10 statements using 1-5 point Likert-type scale. The results were tabulated and analyzed for emergent themes (Williams, 2008). The analysis of students' attitude towards mathematics and science contributed to the understanding of how a structured mentoring program could be designed to encourage more African-American male students to enroll in advanced mathematics and science courses.

Sub-Question 2

What are teacher perceptions and expectations about the enrollment of African-American males in advanced mathematics and science courses?

To answer the survey questions, a total of 20 teachers took an online survey consisting of 10 statements using a 1-5 Likert-type scale with an option for written responses. The responses were also tabulated and analyzed for emergent themes. The purpose of Sub-Question 2 was to determine the perceptions teachers held about African American male students' attitude towards academics in general and mathematics and science subjects in particular. Teacher perceptions informed educators about African Americans regarding the need for dialogue among teachers as well the inclusion of professional development that addresses culturally responsive teaching. A culturally relevant pedagogy was required if teachers were expected to mentor students with diverse backgrounds and prepare them to enroll in challenging mathematics and science courses.

Sub-Question 3

What are the elements of a structured mentoring program suitable for teachers to assume the role of mentors?

For this sub-question, mentors were asked five questions:

1. How successful was the intervention?
2. What challenges did you encounter with your mentee(s)?
3. How do you plan to best manage such challenges in the future?
4. What is your opinion about implementing a structured mentoring program for African-American males in this school?
5. What mentoring strategies were particularly useful in your interaction with your mentee?

With the exception of Question 4, the other questions were particularly relevant in determining the elements of a structured mentoring program suitable for teachers to serve as mentors.

Sub-Question 4

What is the impact of a school-based mentoring program on the academic outcome of African-American male high school students?

To answer Sub-Question 4, analyses of the responses to Interview Question 4 gave insight into understanding the impact of a school-based mentoring program on the academic outcome of African-American male high school students. The responses provided by participating students were analyzed thematically to determine the impact of a school-based mentoring program. Listed are the questions the students were asked:

1. What are some benefits you obtained from your teacher during the intervention (the extra help you received for your teacher in assisting you with mathematics and science)?
2. What are some specific things your teacher did that helped you to improve your grade in mathematics and science?
3. After the extra help your teacher has been providing for you, will you enroll in advanced mathematics and science courses (pre-calculus, calculus, AP chemistry, and AP biology and so on)?
4. After all the help you have been receiving from your teacher, do you still have any doubts about enrolling in advanced mathematics and science courses?
5. Do you think more African-American male students will become interested in enrolling in advanced mathematics and sciences courses if their teachers give them the extra help similar to the help you have been receiving from your teacher?

Limitations of the Research Design

Although the sampling method used was a convenience sample and the participants are representative of a larger population sample, it was limited in that the researcher cannot precisely generalize the results to a larger population (McMillan, 2011). The sample size consisted of 12 students and 20 teachers, which met the approved number of participants, therefore the possibility of new information with additional participants cannot be disregarded (McMillan, 2011). Participatory action research, according to Stringer (2007), involved the inclusion of participants in the entire planning of the methodology. Due to the difficulty of having ample time for teachers to meet and plan an entire methodology, the teachers only gave input by generating a list of strategies used with their assigned mentees.

Credibility, Dependability, Conformability, and Transferability

To ensure credibility, all participants were provided with extended opportunities to explore and experience their individual expertise in the activities, events, and issues related to the problem investigated. For example, mentors demonstrated accountability when they documented their interactions and outcomes with the mentees in the biweekly mentor progress report. The mentor report was one avenue by which participants verified the action research representing their perspectives and experiences.

To ensure dependability and conformability, all measures stated and required for the action research were adhered to and fully documented. The researcher's methodology and all research processes were thoroughly reviewed with several iterations by the Institutional Review Board (IRB) prior to the implementation of the study. The credibility and dependability of the researcher's study incorporated various methods for augmenting the empirical nature of the qualitative research. Shenton (2004) suggested various ways in which this can be done; three were utilized by the researcher. First, frequent debriefing occurred between the researcher and his mentor via e-mail to improve the quality of the study. Telephone conferences provided an avenue for collaboration and discussion of alternative approaches to solving problems. The researcher collaborated with colleagues as informants to evaluate the research project with objectivity and by doing so enabled the researcher to strengthen his position in light of the comments offered. The researcher used thick description to provide detailed analysis of the situation for clarity.

According to Stringer (2007), the outcomes of quantitative or experimental studies could be generalizable to other populations. However, the outcomes of action research may not be generalizable to other people and places due to the unique context of the organization. Transferability was ensured in this unique action research, which clearly stated the specific context in which the research took place at the research site high school. It will be up to the discretion of other researchers to make judgments of replication about whether or not the situation is sufficiently identical to their own organizational context (Stringer, 2007).

Ethical Issues

Researcher's Position Statement

The researcher was a biology teacher whose role in the study was purely investigative with the purpose of improving the academic performance of African-American male high school students at a public school in mathematics and science courses. The researcher conducted an intervention by way of a mentor-mentee program that had the potential for adoption school wide. The action research was collaborative in that participating mentors were involved in the development and creation of strategies the mentors practiced with the mentees. Some teachers hold negative stereotypes about African-American males. However, the researcher was purposively objective, basing the objectivity on conceptual and theoretical frameworks and based all discussions on findings as themes emerged. The researcher suspended subjective judgments pertaining to teacher perceptions about the academic achievement of African-American male high school students to avoid bias and remain objective throughout the study.

Conflict of Interest Assessment

A potential conflict of interest was that the researcher taught at the action research study site high school during the action research, and was therefore within proximity and in some instances, familiar with some of the participants included in the study. Because the majority of the participants knew the researcher was a staff member, the tendency for them to not express their opinions candidly, particularly with the survey questions, could have posed a concern. The potential for researcher bias existed. For example, in getting answers to the research questions, the researcher could have been interested in getting only positive feedback without objectively evaluating the intervention. The researcher took conscientious measures to avoid this bias. For example, identified themes were verified by external experts with experience pertinent to educational research.

Conflict of interests emanating from personal bias and subjectivity were managed in several ways. First, participants answering survey questions were not required to state their names on the survey. Second, the researcher disclosed full details of the dissertation project so participants fully understood the goals and rationale for the study. The participants were informed the researcher's role was purely investigative, and therefore questions were requested to be answered honestly and objectively. Participants were assured of confidentiality and preservation of data (Appendix D and E). The researcher shared findings including analyses of the data with participants.

Ethical Issues in the Study

The researcher is a science teacher at the research site high school and directly interacts with students and all stakeholders. The assumption that African-American male high school students show a lack of interest in their academics that teachers and other stakeholders hold about African-American male high school students was tested and reflected upon. The researcher's role was purely investigative and, therefore, took measures to avoid potential bias and/or conflict of interest throughout the action research.

To eliminate the potential for suspicion or coercion regarding the perceptions or beliefs of the participants, the researcher clearly stated the purpose of the study and assured participants of confidentially. Actual names of participants were not shared with other participants, but were coded in the analyses of the study to protect all participants with anonymity. The proper protocol of informed consent with full disclosure was strictly adhered to. The action research study posed minimal risk because the probability of discomfort and or harm anticipated in the research was not greater than what is normally encountered in daily life for any of the participants.

Chapter 3 Summary

In summary, Chapter 3 highlighted the purpose of this unique action research study, which was to encourage African-American male high school freshmen and sophomores via mentoring intervention to enroll in advanced mathematics and science courses prior to graduation. The researcher investigated the issue using a research design best aligned with the research problem as well as the research questions. The research methodology chosen was a qualitative action research in which both the students and their teachers played an active role in the research process.

The choice of this action research design and its alignment with the research questions was unique and narrowed the gap in the research design literature. Both groups of participants had an opportunity to describe their personal experiences. The experiences were revealed using multiple sources of data including interviews and surveys. All data sets were coded into broad categories and analyzed using emergent theme analysis and thick descriptions via an inductive process.

Each analyzed data set was then further used as a sub-set for comparative analysis and triangulation with other data sub-sets. The researcher ensured credibility, dependability, conformability, and transferability. Ethical issues were addressed by following specific procedures in compliance with the mandates set forth by the Institutional Review Board.

CHAPTER IV
DATA ANALYSIS AND FINDINGS

Introduction

Chapter 4 presented a non-evaluative reporting of the data, supported by tables and where applicable. The chapter is organized into three major sections. First, a detailed description of the sample was discussed. Second, the results of the research methodology and analyses entailing numerical analyses of two sets of surveys revealed the frequency of participants' preferences presented. The data derived from the survey on teacher perceptions about the low enrollment of African-American males was analyzed numerically and thematically for emergent themes. The data derived from two sets of interviews was coded and inductively analyzed thematically for emergent themes. Third, upon analysis of the data sets, a findings summary of each data set was presented. Data sources were then triangulated via comparative analysis to decipher commonalities and differing emergent themes among all data sets. The chapter concluded with a summary of findings and main points providing answers to research questions.

Description of the Sample

The study consisted of 12 African American male students in grades 9 and 10. All 12 students met the inclusion criteria for participation. Each student participant had at least a grade of C at the beginning of the study and scored at least at the basic level in their most recent standardized test score obtained from the school's records on standardized test scores for 2013. Table 1 summarizes the characteristics of the students by grade level, assigned mentor, grade in mathematics at the start and end of the study, and most recent (2013) standardized test score in mathematics. A total of 10 teachers served as mentors, and another set of 10 teachers participated in the online survey. Note that Mentors D004 and F006 appear twice in Table 1 because they mentored two students.

Table 1. Characteristics of African-American Male Student Participants

Mentee	Mentor	Grade Level	Grade in Mathematics at Start of Study	Grade in Mathematics at End of Study	Test Score in Mathematics 2013 – CST Scores	Mathematics course taken at time of study
A1	A001	10	B	B+	proficient	Geometry
B2	B002	9	A	A	proficient	Geometry
C3	C003	9	C	C	basic	Algebra 1
D4	D004	10	C	C+	basic	Algebra 1

Mentee	Mentor	Grade Level	Grade in Mathematics at Start of Study	Grade in Mathematics at End of Study	Test Score in Mathematics 2013 – CST Scores	Mathematics course taken at time of study
E5	D004	10	C	C	basic	Geometry
F6	F006	10	B	B	proficient	Geometry
G7	F006	9	B	B	proficient	Geometry
H8	H008	10	C	C	basic	Algebra 1
I9	I009	10	C	B	basic	Geometry
J10	J010	10	C	B	basic	Geometry
K11	K011	10	B	B	proficient	Algebra 2
L12	L012	10	C	C	proficient	Geometry

Of the 12 African American male students who participated in the study, 10 met the criterion of 20 hours of mentoring. Two of the student mentees (A1 and C3) met with their mentors for only 10 hours, but both participated in the online survey, Mentor C003 and Mentee C3 did not participate in the exit interview due to Mentee C3 opting out of the intervention for athletic reasons.

A total of 10 teachers served as mentors as well as participated in the online survey. Another set of 10 teachers at the same research site participated only in the online survey. All participating teachers belonged to one of the following three ethnic groups: Hispanic, African-American, or Caucasian. Table 2 summarizes the characteristics of the teachers who participated in the study and indicates their ethnicity, years of teaching experience, and sex. Participants A through L served as mentors as well as took the online survey on teacher perceptions towards African-American males in mathematics and science.

Table 2. Mentor Demographics

Mentor	Ethnicity	Years of Teaching Experience	Gender
A001	White	12	male
B002	White	6	male
C003	Hispanic	8	female
D004	African American	12	male
F006	Hispanic	8	male
H008	Hispanic	10	female
I009	Hispanic	13	female
J010	White	10	male
K011	Hispanic	12	female
L012	White	15	female
M013	African American	9	male
N014	African American	12	male
O015	White	12	female
P016	Hispanic	8	female
Q017	African American	13	female
R018	Hispanic	15	female
S019	African American	17	male
T020	White	20	female

Research Design and
Introduction to the Analysis

The design for the study is collaborative action research (Herr & Anderson, 2005). Action research is a type of qualitative research in which action is taken and reflected upon to improve practice. Action research is the most suitable research design for this study that sought to evaluate the effects of strategies to increase the enrollment of African-American males in advanced mathematics and science courses in high school. The intervention is a structured mentoring program in which teachers act as mentors to their students and work with them to improve their mathematics and science skills. Although the research methodology is not fully participatory, it does include the collaborative efforts of the teachers to mentor their students thereby acting to effect change.

The methods used to collect data consisted of two sets of surveys and two sets of interviews. The surveys assessed African-American male students' attitudes towards mathematics and science, and teacher perceptions of African-American male students' attitudes towards the same. Both data were analyzed numerically by computing the average rating for each response from a 1-5 Likert-type scale, as well as the frequencies of the number of respondents per survey statement. The purpose of both surveys was to garner information to assess rather than measure the impact of factors that might influence the performance of African-American males in mathematics and science courses. Thus, although it is not typical to use quantitative data in qualitative action research, these surveys consisting of only 10 statements were vital in evaluating factors that may either impede or enhance the achievement of African-American males in science and mathematics courses. The frequencies of participant responses, in conjunction with the average ratings, were used only for comparative analysis in assessing diversity of the opinions and preferences of the respondents. No other statistical measurements were computed.

The average ratings of the student responses and concurrent frequencies of the student responses to all questions are presented in Data Set 1. The percentage of those surveyed aligns with the most frequent negative rating, and the most positive rating for each question is shown in Table 13. Similarly, the data on teacher perceptions (Data Set 2) were also analyzed on three levels showing the average ratings of the teacher responses for each question and the frequencies of each response. The percentages of respondents that correspond to the most frequent negative rating and most frequent positive rating are indicated in Table 23. Both sets of analyses were also used to develop a third level of inductive thematic analysis in prose form. Interviews (Data Sets 3 and 4) were analyzed on two levels: a transcript of participant responses coded into broad categories, and an inductive thematic analysis in tabular form (Tables 25-34). All inductive thematic analyses were presented in the summary of findings.

Data Analysis

Tables 3-12 display the results of African-American male students' answers to the Survey Questions 1-10.

Table 3. Science is Boring to Me Because ...

Responses	Frequency of Responses	Number of Responses (%)
I am not interested in science.	25	3
My teachers don't make science interesting.	16.67	2
Science is not as exciting as sports.	16.67	2
I don't see how science will help me in life.	0.	0
Science is not boring to me.	41.67	5
Total	12	12
Average rating	3.17	

Table 4. Math is Boring to Me Because ...

Responses	Frequency of Responses	Number of Responses (%)
I am not interested in math.	0	0
My teachers don't make math interesting.	16.67	2
Math is not as exciting as sports.	16.67	2
I don't see how math will help me in life.	0.	0
Mathis not boring to me.	66.67	8
Total	12	12
Average rating	4.17	

Table 5. I Plan on Enrolling in at Least Pre-Calculus and One Advanced Placement Science Subject Before I Graduate

Scale	Frequency of Responses	Number of Responses (%)
Least Agree	8.33	1
Somewhat Disagree	16.67	2
Neither Agree or Disagree	25	3
Somewhat Agree	8.33	1
Strongly Agree	41.67	5
Total	12	12
Average rating	3.58	

Table 6. I Plan to Major in a Math or Science Course When I Go to College

Scale	Frequency of Responses	Number of Responses (%)
Least Agree	33.33	4
Somewhat Disagree	0	0
Neither Agree or Disagree	16.67	2
Somewhat Agree	8.33	1
Strongly Agree	41.67	5
Total	12	12
Average rating	3.25	

Table 7. If I Have a Mentor (Someone Who Helps Me Regularly), I Will Have Good Grades in Science and Math

Scale	Frequency of Responses	Number of Responses (%)
Least Agree	0	0
Somewhat Disagree	8.33	1
Neither Agree or Disagree	41.67	5
Somewhat Agree	8.33	1
Strongly Agree	41.67	5
Total	12	12
Average rating	3.83	

Table 8. Taking Advanced Math Courses, such as Calculus, AP Science, and AP Biology, Will Help Me Succeed in College

Scale	Frequency of Responses	Number of Responses (%)
Least Agree	0	0
Somewhat Disagree	16.67	2
Neither Agree or Disagree	33.33	4
Somewhat Agree	8.33	1
Strongly Agree	41.67	5
Total	12	12
Average rating	3.75	

Table 9. I Do Not Want to Take Any More Mathematics and Science Courses in my Junior or Senior Year than the Minimum Required

Scale	Frequency of Responses	Number of Responses (%)
Least Agree	41.67	5
Somewhat Disagree	0	0
Neither Agree or Disagree	33.33	4
Somewhat Agree	8.33	1
Strongly Agree	16.67	2
Total	12	12
Average rating	1.83	

Table 10. I Do Not Plan to Take Calculus and AP Courses Because Most African-American Males Are Not Usually Enrolled in These Courses

Scale	Frequency of responses (%)	Number of responses
Least Agree	58.33	7
Somewhat Disagree	16.67	2
Neither Agree or Disagree	8.33	1
Somewhat Agree	16.67	2
Strongly Agree	0	0
Total	12	12
Average rating	1.83	

Table 11. Science Is Challenging to Me Because ...

Scale	Frequency of Responses	Number of Responses (%)
There is no one at home to help me.	0	0
My teachers don't give me any extra help.	8.33	1
I can get help, but I am just not into science.	16.67	3
I like science, but the tests are difficult.	33.33	4
I like science, and I don't find it challenging.	33.33	4

Scale	Frequency of Responses	Number of Responses (%)
Total	12	12
Average rating	3.92	

Table 12. Math Is Challenging to Me Because ...

Responses	Frequency of Responses	Number of Responses (%)
My math teacher does not believe in me.	0	0
I love math, but the tests are hard.	16.67	2
There is no one at home to help me.	8.67	1
I can understand the concept if my teacher explains better.	25	3
I like math, and it is not challenging to me.	50	6
Total	12	12
Average rating	4.08	

Data Set 1. Average Ratings of Student Responses and Concurrent Frequencies

Table 13. African American Male Students' Attitude Towards Mathematics and Science by Average, Most Frequent Negative, and Most Frequent Positive Ratings

Survey Statement number	Average Rating	Most frequent negative rating (%)	Response no. of most frequent negative rating	Most frequent positive rating (%)	Response no. of most frequent positive rating
1	3.17	25	1	41.67	5
2	4.17	16.67	2,3	66.67	5
3	3.58	16.67	2	41.67	5

Survey Statement number	Average Rating	Most frequent negative rating (%)	Response no. of most frequent negative rating	Most frequent positive rating (%)	Response no. of most frequent positive rating
4	3.25	33.3	1	41.67	5
5	3.83	8.33	2	41.67	5
6	3.75	16.67	2	41.67	5
7	2.58	16.67	5	41.67	1
8	1.83	16.67	2	58.33	5
9	3.92	25	3	33.33	4
10	4.08	NA	NA	50.00	5

Data Set 2. Analysis of Survey on Teacher Perception of African American Male Students' Attitudes Toward Mathematics and Science

Table 14. Most African-American males in This School Tend to Limit Themselves, and Therefore May Not Enroll in Advanced Courses in Science and Mathematics

Responses	Frequency of Responses	Number of Responses (%)
Negative peer pressure	26.32	5
They don't see many of their peers taking on challenging courses in science and math	26.32	5
They do not see any value in taking challenging math and science courses	36.84	7
Some teachers hold low expectations of them	10.53	2
Other	0	0
Total		19
Average rating	2.32	

Table 15. Most African-American males Are More Concerned About Sports and Entertainment Than Pursuing Mathematics and Science Related Careers

Responses	Frequency of Responses	Number of Responses (%)
Because the media portrays many Black males in sports and entertainment	40	8
They are not familiar with the gains of mathematics and science related jobs	20	4
Sports and entertainment are easier to attain than academics	15	3
Lack of parental involvement and mentoring	20	4
Other	5	1
Total		20
Average rating	2.30	

Table 16. The Media Hardly Ever Portray Images of African-American males in Career Other Than Sports and Entertainment

Scale	Frequency of responses (%)	Number of responses
Least Agree	0	0
Somewhat Disagree	5	1
Neither Agree or Disagree	40	8
Somewhat Agree	35	7
Strongly Agree	20	4
Total		20
Average rating	3.70	

Table 17. Some Teachers Seldom Motivate African-American males to Take on Challenging Courses Such as Advanced Mathematics and AP Science Courses Because ...

Responses	Frequency of Responses	Number of Responses (%)
Some hold low expectations of them	31.58	6
Some teachers don't have the extra time to mentor students	0	0
Some African American students	42.11	8

Responses	Frequency of Responses	Number of Responses (%)
exhibit an "I don't care" attitude		
Other	26.32	5
Total		19
Average rating	2.63	

Table 18. Teachers Will Be Better Able to Instruct African-American Males to Succeed and Enroll in Advanced Mathematics and Science if They Are Trained on Effective Academic Mentoring Strategies

Scale	Frequency of responses (%)	Number of responses
Least Agree	11.11	2
Somewhat Disagree	5.56	1
Neither Agree or Disagree	22.22	4
Somewhat Agree	33.33	6
Strongly Agree	27.78	5
Total		18
Average rating	3.61	

Table 19. Successfully Monitoring the Progress of African-American Males in Mathematics and Science Since Elementary School Serves as a Viable Strategy for Them to Succeed in These Subjects in High School

Scale	Frequency of responses (%)	Number of responses
Least Agree	0	0
Somewhat Disagree	0	0
Neither Agree or Disagree	21.05	4
Somewhat Agree	31.58	6
Strongly Agree	47.37	9
Total		10
Average rating	4.26	

Table 20. *The School Does Not Adequately Guide African-American*
males to Enroll in Advanced Mathematics and Science Courses
Because ...

Responses	Frequency of Responses	Number of Responses (%)
Counselors don't act to change the low enrollment data of African-American males in these courses	5.56	1
Some African American parents are not involved in making sure their students are enrolled in these courses	50	9
Teachers hardly ever play the role of mentors and track the placement of African-American males in these courses	0	0
Counselors hold low expectations of African-American males	0	0
Other	44.44	8
Total		18
Average rating	3.28	

Table 21. *Who Do You Think is Responsible for the Academic Success*
of African-American Males in Mathematics and Science Related
Courses

Responses	Frequency of Responses	Number of Responses (%)
Parents	21.05	4
Society	0	0
The school	0	0
Parents, society, and the school	42.11	8
Other	36.84	7
Total		19
Average rating	3.74	

Table 22. Assigning African-American males with a Mentor Will Increase Their Chances of Staying Focused in Their Academics Including Enrollment in Advanced Mathematics and Science

Scale	Frequency of responses (%)	Number of responses
Least Agree	0	0
Somewhat Disagree	5.26	1
Neither Agree or Disagree	47.37	9
Somewhat Agree	21.05	4
Strongly Agree	26.32	5
Total		19
Average rating	3.68	

Table 23. Counselors Must Ensure That African-American males Are Properly Guided into Taking Advanced Courses in Mathematics and Science

Scale	Frequency of responses (%)	Number of responses
Least Agree	5.26	1
Somewhat Disagree	5.26	1
Neither Agree or Disagree	26.32	5
Somewhat Agree	26.32	5
Strongly Agree	36.84	7
Total		19
Average rating	3.84	

Data Set 2. Analysis 2

Table 24. Analysis of Survey on Teacher Perceptions of African-American Males' Attitude Towards Mathematics and Science

Survey statement number	Average rating (%)	Most frequent Rating (%)	Most frequent rating response number	Least frequent Rating (%)	Least frequent rating response number
1	NA	36.84%	5	0%	5
2	NA	40%	5	5%	5

Survey statement number	Average rating (%)	Most frequent Rating (%)	Most frequent rating response number	Least frequent Rating (%)	Least frequent rating response number
3	3.58	40%	5	5%	1
4	NA	42.11%	5	26.32%	2
5	3.83	33.3%	4	5.5%	2
6	4.25	47.37%	4	0%	1,2
7	NA	50%	2	0%	3 and 4
8	3.74	42.11%	4	0%	2 and 3
9	3.68	47.37%	3	5.26%	4
10	3.84	36.84%	5	5.26%	1 and 2

Note. Not Applicable (NA) refers to survey statements that have a variety of word choices.

Data Set 3. Analysis of Post Intervention Interviews with Mentees

Question 1. What are some benefits you obtained from your teacher?

Categories.

Academic help.

"I learned how to solve various problems involving similar triangles." (Mentee B2)
"I retained much knowledge from my teacher – she gave extra tutoring." (Mentee K11)
"I was able to get better at my reading and writing." (Mentee L12)

"When I don't understand a concept, I call my teacher for help." (Mentee J10)

"We will have tutoring and special help during class." (Mentee G7)

Coming to tutoring on a daily basis really helps." (Mentee F6)

"It helped me with my grade and work skills." (Mentee H8)

Motivation.

"Pep talks and motivation." (Mentee K11)

"Concentrate better and focus more." (Mentee D4)

"It helped me get my life in the right direction" (Mentee E5)

Question 2. What are some specific things your teacher did that helped you improve your grade in mathematics and science?

Categories.

Accountability.

"My teacher would bug me about doing the work and make sure it's done correctly." (Mentee E5)

Extended opportunity.

"My teacher helped me improve my grade by letting me retake quizzes." (Mentee J10)

"She let me retake test and help me fix my grade."
(Mentee I9)

Clarifying concepts.

"My teacher will help me with problems I did not
understand." (Mentee G7)
"My teacher has helped me with multiple ways to
understand the quadratic formula." (Mentee F6)
"He helped me with finding the lengths of complex
triangles and the angles of intersection." (Mentee B2)
"She sat me down and helped me understand the
material." (Mentee K11)

Question 3. After the extra help your teacher
has been providing for you, will you enroll in
advanced mathematics and science courses (pre-
calculus, calculus, AP chemistry, AP Biology and so
on)?

Categories.

*Enrollment in advanced mathematics and science –
positive.*

"Yes, I will enroll in advanced math and science
courses." (Mentee L12)
"I most likely will next year or my senior year."
(Mentee E5)
"I will enroll in Algebra 2 honors." (Mentee J10)
"Yes, I will." (Mentee G7)

"Yes, I will go into pre-calculus." (Mentee B2)
"Yes, I will be enrolling in pre-calculus honors and AP calculus." (Mentee K11)
"Yes, my teacher recommends that I enroll in these classes." (Mentee F6)

Enrollment in advanced mathematics and science – negative.

"No, I am going to stay in my regular classes." (Mentee D4)
"Nothing, because I believe my career won't be in math and science." (Mentee L12)

Question 4. After all the help you have been receiving from your teacher, do you still have any doubts about enrolling in advanced mathematics and science courses?

Categories.

Doubts.

"Yes I do still have doubts about math and science." (Mentee L12)
"I feel as though I am not ready, but if I stay focused it will be fine." (Mentee F6)
"I do not plan to take advance courses in math and science." (Mentee D4)
I have a little bit of doubt in it maybe I won't be fast enough to get in the work as other students." (Mentee E5)

"Yes, because math is not my strongest subject."
(Mentee I9)
"I think I still need help in Algebra." (Mentee H8)

No doubts.

"No." (Mentee K11)
"No, I think I will go into more advanced classes."
(Mentee B2)
"No, not really." (Mentee J10)
"No, I will enroll in advanced math and science
courses." (Mentee G7)

Question 5. Do you think more African-American male students will become interested in enrolling in advanced mathematics and science courses if their teachers give them the extra help similar to the help you have been receiving from your teacher?

Categories.

Extra help by teachers as sole determinant of enrollment in advanced mathematics and science – in favor of the premise.

"Yes, as long as the classes are not too difficult for them." (Mentee B2)
"I think they might it depends on the mentor." (Mentee D4)
"Yes, I think it should start in a younger age at elementary school to interest them." (Mentee F6)

"I believe most of them will if they truly understood why school is important." (Mentee E5)
"Yes, I think you just have to interest them at a young age like I was." (Mentee G7)
"Yes, I think so because if they get extra help they will assume they will pass the class." (Mentee J10)
"If they have great help and try to like it, they will." (Mentee I9)

Extra help by teachers as sole determinant of enrollment in advanced mathematics and science – against the premise.

"No, the teacher can only do so much but if the student doesn't have self-motivation to succeed then they won't." (Mentee K11)
"I am not sure if other students would be interested in math and science courses." (Mentee L12)

Data Set 4. Post Intervention Interview Questions with Mentors

Question 1. How successful was the intervention?

Category.

Successful intervention.

"Student continues to be successful in both math and science classes." (Mentor A001)

"It was reasonably successful. Retaking quizzes helped his grade." (Mentor J010)
"I feel that the intervention was successful. He is a good student." (Mentor K011)
"The intervention seemed to help build B2's math and science skills." (Mentor B002)
"It was more successful tutoring him in math than in science." (Mentor H008)
"This intervention was very successful; without this intervention F6 would have failed this semester." (Mentor F006)

Question 2. What challenges did you encounter with your mentee?

Category.

Challenges.

"Student lacks follow through with research assignments." (Mentor A001)
"Meeting times were hard to keep up." (Mentor A001)
"Finding time to meet was hard for us sometimes." (Mentor J010)
"Keeping F6 focused was difficult; I had to redirect him often." (Mentor F006)
"Scheduling tutoring session was hard sometimes." (Mentor F006)
"It was hard to keep mentees motivated." (Mentor D004)
"He is very reserved and difficult to get him to talk about his aspirations." (Mentor L012)

"I did not encounter any challenges; the hardest part was finding time." (Mentor K011)

Question 3. How do you plan to best manage such challenges in the future?

Category.

Managing challenges.

"Persistence and real life connections seemed to spark conversation with him." (Mentor L012)
"I feel that the intervention will be more successful if we are given more time." (Mentor K011)
"Next year I will be freer to meet with mentee in the morning." (Mentor I009)
"I feel making a set schedule could benefit this student." (Mentor H008)
"Continue to request student to see me after school." (Mentor A001)
"Set and stick to clearly defined times." (Mentor J010)
"In the future, I could tutor students during lunch." (Mentor F006)
"I could give the student a mock test the day before an actual test to see where his misconceptions are." (Mentor F006)

Question 4. What is your opinion about implementing a structured mentoring program for African-American males in this school?

Category.

Implement a structured mentoring program.

"I have been asking for this type of program for our math department for years, but our administrator says that we cannot make after school tutoring mandatory. I beg to differ." (Mentor F006)
"I think it will be very helpful as students are being closely monitored and making sure they are enrolled in the right courses for college and career readiness." (Mentor L012)
"I feel a program like this is can be successful with all kinds of students, not just African-American males." (Mentor K011)
"I believe it is necessary to bridge the gap. It is very difficult to motivate certain students; however, anything to provide support and accommodations is a good start." (Mentor B002)
"I think that a structured mentoring program for African-American males in this school would be highly beneficial." (Mentor H008)
"I feel, however, that mentoring for males should be conducted by males for the purpose of male bonding." (Mentor H008)

Question 5. What mentoring strategies were particularly useful in your interaction with your mentee?

Category.

Useful mentoring strategies.

"Having mentee investigates things that spark his interest." (Mentor H008)

"One-on-one talking about classroom experiences seemed to relax student about school more." (Mentor A001)

"One strategy is researching college expectations." (Mentor A001)

"Looking into famous African-American people." (Mentor A001)

"Major research about what it takes to prepare for college." (Mentor D004)

"Just spending time one-on-one and focusing on the student's specific need." (Mentor J010)

"Consistent meetings and reflections on what was accomplished." (Mentor L012)

"I think that pep talks with the student and reflecting on his progress motivated the student a lot more." (Mentor K011)

"One-on-one instructing and tutoring worked well. Discussions were good as well." (Mentor B002)

"Tutoring and having mentee make up missed homework assignments." (Mentor F006)

Summary of Findings

Data Set 1

Data Set 1 was created to investigate attitudes participating African-American male students hold towards mathematics and science. The various themes included in the investigation were: (a) interest, (b) possibility of enrollment in advanced mathematics and science in high school and college, (c) mentoring, (d) advanced mathematics and science as courses necessary for college readiness, and (e) perceived difficulty in mathematics and science. The average rating for respondents' interest in science (i.e., science is not boring) and mathematics was 3.17 and 4.17 respectively, with a relatively lower interest in science than in mathematics (41.67% versus 66.67% respectively).

The average rating for possibility of enrollment in advanced mathematics and science in high school and majoring in those courses in college was 3.58 and 3.25 respectively, with the highest rating of 41.67% consistency in enrollment at both the high school and college level. The result of this survey was also consistent with the results pertaining to taking more mathematics and science courses in junior and senior years in high school in that 41.67% of respondents strongly agreed they would enroll in those years.

The average rating for mentoring as an intervention to improve grades in science and mathematics was a 3.8, indicating agreement. The highest rating was 41.67% tied for Choices 3 and 5. The need for enrolling in advanced mathematics and science courses to be 'college ready' received an average rating of 3.75, indicating agreement for this need. Regarding the influences of their peers, 58.33% of respondents indicated their peers had no influence in their decision to enroll in advanced mathematics and science courses. The highest percentage rating for difficulty in science (i.e., science is challenging) was 33%, tied for Choices 4 and 5. The highest percentage rating for difficulty in mathematics was at 50% for Choice 5 (math was not challenging).

Data Set 2

The purpose of Data Set 2 was to investigate teacher perceptions about African-American male students' attitudes towards mathematics and science to understand factors possibly contributing to low enrollment of African-American male students at the research site. The results of the survey were analyzed thematically based on the most frequent choices of the survey statements. Two categories emerged from the analysis: the causes of low enrollment of African-American males in advanced mathematics and science and the intervention. These themes emerged in the first category: worthwhileness (i.e., students' familiarity with gains of science and mathematics), negative peer pressure, media, lack of parent involvement, teacher stereotypes and biases, students' attitudes (i.e., lack of interest), and other stakeholders.

For the second category, intervention, these themes emerged professional development for teachers specifically in mentoring strategies and early mentoring for students in elementary school.

Data Set 3. Summary of the Findings of Interviews Conducted with Mentees

Question 1. What are some benefits you obtained from your teacher during the intervention (the extra help you received from your teacher in assisting you with mathematics and science)?

Table 25. Data Set 3, Question 1

Category	Thematic Category	Key Terms	Characteristic
Benefit 1	Academic help	Concept, help, tutoring	When the teacher gives extra help students understand the concepts better.
Benefit 2	Motivation	Pep talks, focus, direction	Mentor-mentee interaction motivates students to focus on learning.

Question 2. What are some specific things your teacher did that helped you to improve your grade in mathematics and science?

Table 26. Data Set 3, Question 2

Category	Thematic Category	Key Terms	Characteristic
Teaching Strategy 1	Account-ability	Bug me, done	The teacher persists in ensuring students complete their work.
Teaching Strategy 2	Extended opportunity	Improve, retake	When the teachers give students an opportunity to retake a test, the students improve their grades.
Teaching Strategy 3	Clarifying Concepts	Understand, difficult, multiple	Teachers can help students with multiple ways to understand difficult concepts.

Question 3. After the extra help your teacher has been providing for you, will you enroll in advanced mathematics and science courses?

Table 27. Data Set 3, Question 3

Category	Thematic Category	Key Terms	Characteristic
Enroll-ment 1	Plan to enroll in advanced mathematics and science courses	Advanced mathematics, science, yes	Eight students' participants indicated they would enroll.
Enroll-ment 2	No plan to enroll in advanced mathematics and science	No	Two student participants do not plan to enroll.

Question 4. After all the extra help you have been receiving from your teacher, do you still have any doubts about enrolling in advanced mathematics and science courses?

Table 28. Data Set 3, Question 4

Category	Thematic Category	Key Terms	Characteristic
Aspiration fo increased enrollment 1	Doubts	Maybe	About half the students had apprehensions about wanting to enroll.
Aspiration of increased enrollment 2	No Doubts	No, I will	The other half of the students indicated with certainty that they will enroll.

Question 5. Do you think more African-American male students will become interested in enrolling in advanced mathematics and science courses if their teachers give them the extra help similar to the help you have been receiving from your teacher?

Table 29. Data Set 3, Question 5

Category	Thematic Category	Key Terms	Characteristic
Extra Help 1	Interest	Interested, like, motivation	Although teachers could give students extra help, the students themselves must be self-motivated to engage in advanced mathematics and science courses.
Extra Help 2	Early Intervention	Younger age	Mentoring students at start of elementary school increases the likelihood they would enroll in rigorous mathematics and science courses in high school

Data Set 4. Summary of the Findings of the Interviews Conducted with Mentors

Question 1. How successful was the intervention?

Table 30. Data Set 4, Question 1

Category	Thematic Category	Key Terms	Characteristic
Evaluation of intervention 1	Successful	Success, grades	Mentoring African American male students was a successful intervention
Evaluation of intervention 2	Improved mathematics and science skills	Mathematics, science, skill	One outcome of mentoring was improved skills and grades in mathematics and science.

Question 2. What challenges did you encounter with your mentee?

Table 31. Data Set 4, Question 2

Category	Thematic Category	Key Terms	Characteristic
Challenges 1	Time management	Time	Although mentors did meet with mentees, scheduling time to meet was difficult.
Challenges 2	Motivation	Follow through, focus	Some mentors had difficulty keeping mentees focused.

Question 3. How do you plan to best manage such challenges in the future?

Table 32. Data Set 4, Question 3

Category	Thematic Category	Key Terms	Characteristic
Managing challenges	Fixed schedule	Time	Mentors must set a clearly defined time by which to meet with mentees.

Question 4. What is your opinion about implementing a structured mentoring program for African-American males in this school?

Table 33. Data Set 4, Question 4

Category	Thematic Category	Key Terms	Characteristic
Opinion 1	Academic support	Support, helpful	A structured mentoring program provides academic support to students.
Opinion 2	Tracking	Monitor, college, career	A structured mentoring program ensures that mentee is guided into taking the right classes for college and career readiness.

Question 5. What mentoring strategies were particularly useful in your interaction with your mentee?

Table 34. Data Set 4, Question 5

Category	Thematic Category	Key Terms	Characteristic
Mentoring Strategies 1	Specific needs	One-on-one, tutoring	One-on-one tutoring and instructing students caters to their specific needs.

Category	Thematic Category	Key Terms	Characteristic
Mentoring Strategies 2	Reflection	Reflecting, discussion	One-on-one discussion with mentees about their classroom experiences helps the students to relax.

Triangulation of Data Sets

Common emergent themes arose from the data sets including mentoring, interest, and monitoring progress.

Mentoring. The influence of mentoring at an early age as a viable strategy received the highest ratings in all data sets indicating a preference for this strategy.

Interest. Although mentoring is desired, all data sets indicated that students must be self-motivated to improve their science and mathematics skills.

Monitoring progress. All data sets indicated that tracking the progress of mentees would ensure students enrolled in classes such as advanced mathematics and science in order for them to be college and career ready.

There was disparity in the findings of the survey on students' attitudes towards science and mathematics compared to teacher perceptions about students' attitudes towards these two subjects. On the one hand, students' attitudinal surveys indicated that about half the participating students showed reasonable positive attitudes towards science and mathematics. All survey questions pertaining to interests in science and mathematics and enrollment in these subjects in their junior and senior years in high school as well as in college, received the highest ratings. On the other hand, 42.11% of teachers indicated that African-American males exhibit an, *I don't care attitude.*

Summary

Chapter 4 highlighted the analysis of all data sets obtained from the participants in the study. Two sets of surveys and two sets of interviews were analyzed. A survey on African American male students' perception was numerically analyzed computing the average ratings and frequencies of the responses. The survey of teacher perception of low enrollment of African-American males in advanced mathematics and science courses was analyzed both numerically and thematically to identify characteristics in the various themes. The results of interviews with mentees and mentors were first analyzed using broad categories, followed by inductive thematic analysis. All data sets were triangulated via a comparative analysis to inductively determine common and differing themes.

The following are the research questions and a summary of the findings, which provided insight into answering the research question.

Sub-Question 1. What attitudes do African American male students hold toward mathematics and science courses? Findings indicated about half the African-American male participants tended to show positive attitudes towards mathematics and science indicated by average ratings of 3.17 and 4.17 respectively.

Sub-Question 2. What are teacher perceptions and expectations about the enrollment of African-American males in advanced mathematics and science courses? Findings indicated teachers attributed low enrollment of African-American males to unfamiliarity with gains in science and mathematics, negative peer pressure, media, lack of parental involvement, teacher stereotypes and biases, students' attitudes (i.e., lack of interest), and a lack of support from other stakeholders.

Sub-Question 3. What are the elements of a structured mentoring program suitable for teachers to assume the role of mentors? Findings from the results of interviews indicated teachers as mentors must demonstrate effective time-management, ability to set a fixed schedule with mentee, ability to provide academic support, ability to cater to mentee's specific needs, and reflectivity in their practice.

Sub-Question 4. What is the impact of a school-based mentoring program on the academic outcome of African-American male high school students? Findings from the interviews with both mentees and mentors indicated a school-based mentoring program provided academic support and the ability to monitor mentee's progress, which ultimately resulted in improved grades.

CHAPTER V
CONCLUSIONS AND DISCUSSIONS

Introduction

The overarching purpose of this study was to evaluate the effects of strategies to increase the enrollment of African-American males in advanced mathematics and science courses at a public high school located in southern California. To evaluate the effects of these strategies, an intervention was required. A structured mentoring program was implemented in which participating teachers acted as mentors to one or two students. A qualitative action research design was conducted for the study. Mentors contributed to the design of a biweekly progress report, which consisted of a list of strategies that guided their interactions with mentees. Surveys and interviews were the main sources of data collected from the participants.

This chapter presents a detailed discussion of the study and is organized into nine sub-sections: (a) Summary of the Findings, (b) Discussion of the Findings, (c) Discussion of the Findings in Relation to the Literature, (d) Relationship between the Findings and the Theoretical Framework, (e) Relationship between the Results and the Literature Reviewed, (f) Limitations of the Study, (g) Implication of the

Findings for Practice, (h) Recommendations for Further Research, and (i) a final summary of the answers to the research questions.

Summary of the Findings

The central research question was, "Can a structured mentoring program increase enrollment of African-American males in advanced mathematics and science courses in high school?" To find answers to the central question, sub-research questions were proposed and investigated throughout the study. Answers to the sub-questions provided insight and clarity on how mentoring can be a viable intervention.

Sub-Question 1

What attitudes do African American male students hold toward mathematics and science courses?

The findings indicated approximately half of the participating student mentees show reasonable positive attitudes towards mathematics and science. On a 1-5 Likert-type scale, the lowest average rating was 1.83, and the highest average rating was a 4.17. The possibility of African-American males enrolling in advanced mathematics and science courses in high school and college showed average rating of 3.58. Similarly, the need to enroll in advanced sections of mathematics and science subjects received an average rating of 3.75. The assessment of the perception by the students about the difficulty of science and mathematics courses received highest average rating of 4.08. Exactly half of the student mentees surveyed indicated a liking for mathematics, while a third of the students indicated explicitly they like science and do not find it challenging. The average rating for mentoring was at 3.83, denoting reasonable agreement for the mentoring intervention.

A summary of the findings regarding African-American males' attitudes towards mathematics and science courses derived from the interviews (Data Set 3) indicated the following in regards to their likelihood of African-American males to enroll in advanced mathematics and science courses. Of the 12 students interviewed, nine students stated that they will enroll, and two students stated that they would not enroll (Table 27, Enrollment 1 and 2). On the one hand, although more than half the participating student mentees stated that they would enroll, only about half of them stated that they would do so with absolute certainty; the other interested students had some apprehensions. A general attitude of positive aspirations for advanced mathematics and science course enrollment in future school years was evident (Table 28, Aspiration for increased enrollment 1 and 2). However, the survey on teacher perceptions of African-American males' attitude towards mathematics and science courses showed 42% of teacher mentors perceived African-American males exhibited an *I don't care attitude* (see Table 17).

Sub-Question 2

What are teacher perceptions and expectations about the enrollment of African-American males in advanced mathematics and science?

Generally, the findings of the surveys (see Table 21) indicated the majority of the teachers attributed the factors of low enrollment in mathematics and science courses to societal issues such as the media, the school, and lack of parental involvement. The majority of the teachers, however, agreed on mentoring as an early intervention to improve the mathematics and science skills of African-American males.

Sub-Question 3

What are the elements of a structured mentoring program suitable for teachers to assume the role of mentors?

Findings from the survey on teacher perceptions (see Table 18) indicated an average rating of 3.61 denoting professional development on effective academic mentoring strategies is one element of a structured mentoring program. In addition, effective time management, ability to set a fixed schedule with mentee, ability to provide academic support, ability to address mentees specific needs, and reflecting on mentees classroom experiences are elements necessary for teachers to assume the role of mentors (see Tables 31-34).

Sub-Question 4

What is the impact of a school-based mentoring program on the academic outcome of African-American male high school students?

Nine of the 10 teachers interviewed commented they felt the mentoring intervention was successful. Findings obtained from interviews with both mentees and mentors indicated a school-based mentoring program provides academic support, motivation, and monitoring of mentee's progress that ultimately improves student achievement (Tables 25, 29 & 33).

Discussion of the Findings

To increase the enrollment of African-American males in mathematics and science courses at the public high school where the action research was conducted, a structured mentoring program was implemented as an intervention. The findings of the action research, conducted for over the course of 20 sequential hours, revealed diverse factors that either enhance or impede the achievement of participating African-American males in enrolling in advanced mathematics and science courses prior to graduation.

Participating African-American males in the study appreciably (average attitudinal rating of 4.08) showed positive attitudes towards mathematics and science courses in terms of interests in the subjects, level of difficulty, and possibility of enrollment in advanced sections of these courses in high school as well as in a four-year college. These findings are attributed to several emerging themes that contributed to the positive attitudes of African-American males towards mathematics and science (see Data Set 3). First, student mentees were asked about the benefits they received from the intervention. Student mentees responded with the following remarks in reference to the following key areas.

Academic help. When the teacher gives extra help, students understand the concepts better. For example, Mentee J10 commented, "When I don't understand a concept, I call my teacher for help." Similarly, Mentee F6 noted, "Coming to tutoring on a daily basis really helps." Although it is not the intent of the study to compare grades at the start and end of the study, the students noted in their geometry class Mentee F6 maintained a B and Mentee J10 improved from a C to a B. The maintenance and improvement of student mentees' grades respectively could have been enhanced by the extra assistance they received from their teachers.

Motivation. Mentor-mentee interactions motivated students to focus on learning. As an illustration, Mentee K11 and Mentee D4 noted respectively, "pep talks and motivation" and "concentrate better and focus more." The researcher asked student mentees to comment on specific things (strategies) their teachers did that helped improve their grades. Three themes emerged namely: accountability, extended opportunity, and clarifying concepts.

Accountability. The teacher persists in ensuring students complete their work. One comment by Mentee E5 illustrates this point, "My teacher would bug me about the doing the work and make sure it's done correctly."

Extended opportunity. When the teacher gives students an opportunity to retake a test, the students improve their grades. For instance, Mentee I9 commented, "She lets me retake test and help me fix my grade."

Clarifying concepts. Teachers can help students with multiple ways to understand. A comment made by Mentee G7 illustrates this theme; "My teacher will help me with problems I did not understand."

Two mentees (see Table 1, Mentee H8 and Mentee D4) were particularly resolute in their opinions and demonstrated minimal interest in pursuing advanced mathematics and science courses; either because they lacked motivation or because they found the tests difficult, needing further clarification from their teachers. Table 1, Column 5 indicates both student mentees did not perform better than a grade of C during the intervention. The teacher mentors of Mentee H8 and Mentee D4 attributed the lack of motivation to the absence of early mathematics intervention from elementary school.

The researcher, who is a biology teacher at the research site high school, attests to issues of high failure rates in science and mathematics courses. Students struggle with understanding of the concepts, thereby making it difficult for them to do well on tests. These findings are consistent with research on mentoring as an intervention to improve the academic achievement of students in general. The researcher has observed the usual intervention is to assign struggling students to an after school-tutoring program, which poses the problem of one instructor dealing with a group of approximately five students compared to a 1:1 or 2:1 ratio using a mentoring intervention.

Mentoring relationships produce positive academic outcomes (Ryzin, 2010). Ryzin posited that teacher-student relationships are important to student outcomes in secondary school. Such relationships enable the mentor to maximize the academic potential of the mentee, and thereby leading to an increase in academic achievement. The findings of the Ryzin study parallels the successful outcomes of mentoring posited by the current study. Similarly, an impact study of Big Brothers Big Sisters school-based mentoring program conducted with 10 cities nationwide found mentored students ages 9-16 years old improved their academic performance and developed greater confidence in their academic abilities (Herrera, Grossman, Kauh, & McMaken, 2011). Although the mentors were outside adults (not the teachers of the students), the outcome of mentoring by the Big Brothers and Big Sisters program yielded positive academic outcomes for student mentees.

The findings of the teacher survey were similar to the expected findings of the Ryzin (2010) and Herrera et al. (2011) studies. The findings supported that African-American males are responsible for their own learning in addition to other contributing factors such as parental involvement, media, and negative peer pressure. The findings of these factors are consistent with the abundance of deficit-based research.

The results of the mentoring intervention indicate mentoring African-American males improves their science and mathematics skills. This research study's finding is contrary to the opinion of some of the responses on the survey on teacher perception. For example, for Question 4 (Data Set 2) one teacher mentor commented, "Performance in class should be the only determining factor in AP placement." Performance should be a determining factor; the participant did not state the role that mentoring can play in improving performance. It is evident some teachers hold assumptions that should be re-examined in light of the positive outcome pertaining to student mentoring as a viable intervention to increase the academic success of African-American male high school students in mathematics and science courses.

Teachers should be equipped with the necessary elements to assume the role of mentors. Several themes emerged regarding elements of a structured mentoring program including effective teaching strategies as shown in Table 26. The following key themes are salient to a structured mentoring program.

Time management and fixed schedule. Scheduling time to meet with student mentees was difficult for all mentors. Mentor J010, whose student mentee visited the classroom during lunch and after school, commented, "Finding time to meet was hard sometimes." To mitigate this challenge, Mentor J010 promised to maintain standard times stating, "Set and stick to a fixed schedule." Another (Mentor I009) addressed the issue commenting, "Next year I will be freer to meet with mentee in the morning." Evidently, mentors can be flexible in meeting with mentees; however, one way to resolve the issue is to mutually agree on a specific time to meet.

Academic support. A structured mentoring program provides academic support to students. This theme mirrors that of academic assistance. What was profound about the benefits of the mentoring program was the opportunity to dialogue about the need for implementation of the program. Mentor F006 was particularly enthusiastic when he commented, "I have been asking for this type of program for our math department for many years, but our administrator said we cannot make after school program mandatory – I beg to differ." Mentor F006 was aware of the importance of providing extra academic support; however, not making after school tutoring mandatory limits the number of students available to work with.

After-school tutoring is just one component of the mentoring program, and other strategies can be utilized in mentoring African-American males.

Monitoring African-American males' academic pathway. This strategy ensures mentees are enrolled in college preparatory courses in mathematics and science. This strategy would be a concerted effort of mentors, counselors, parents, and administrators. The following comment by Mentor L012 illustrates the importance of monitoring the course-taking trajectory of mentees: "I think it will be helpful as students are being monitored and making sure they are enrolled in the right courses for college and career readiness." Findings of the mentoring intervention revealed nine of the 12 African American male participants commented in the interview that they would enroll in advanced mathematics and science courses prior to graduation despite the fact some students in the study stated they are apprehensive about enrolling in the more academically challenging classes.

Reflecting on mentees classroom experiences. Another finding revealed one-on-one tutoring, and discussion with student mentees about their classroom experiences, helped the students to relax. Teacher mentors found a way to connect with student mentees by providing opportunities for dialogue. The following comments best illustrated this strategy: "Just spending time one-on-one and focusing on the student's specific need ..." (Mentor J010), and "Consistent meetings and reflections on what was accomplished ..." (Mentor L012). Although teachers may be overwhelmed with too much work, spending time with promising African-American male students and engaging them in conversations about their classroom experiences yielded gains that motivated the students to be academically successful.

Overall, based on the findings of the study, a school-based mentoring program yielded positive academic outcomes for African-American male students. When students have the extra support in mathematics and science courses, they are motivated to improve their skills; thereby, increasing the likelihood they will enroll in advanced mathematics and science courses prior to graduation from high school. A structured mentoring program is one avenue to bridge the enrollment gap in advanced mathematics and science courses between African-American males and their counterparts of other sub-groups. Mentor B002 supported this latter assertion when he commented, "I believe it is necessary to bridge the gap. It is very difficult to motivate certain students; however, anything to provide support and accommodations is a good start." Although mentors were faced with some challenges such as setting a fixed schedule to meet with their mentees; all mentors stated the mentoring program was a successful intervention because the mentors either observed gains in the mentees' mathematics and science skills or helped mentees become focused in developing their (students) mathematics and science skills.

Discussion of the Findings in
Relation to the Literature

This action research study was based on theories of organizational learning (double-loop versus single-loop learning, and Model 1 versus Model 11 thinking), participatory action research, and systems thinking. The findings of the study resonate with these theories and concepts. First, teachers as mentors modeled double-loop learning in that another approach, mentoring, was used in finding solutions to the problem. They demonstrated Model 11 thinking by agreeing to participate in the study giving them an opportunity to question their beliefs and assumptions of the targeted sub group (Argyris & Schon, 2009).

Moreover, the findings indicated the mentoring intervention provided an opportunity for teachers as mentors to have informal dialogue with their mentees during which several interactions occurred. Some examples of the interaction included mentees' reflection on their classroom experiences, mentors' reflection on the progress mentees made during the mentoring intervention, and mentors discussed with mentee the advantages of enrolling in advanced mathematics and science courses.

Second, teacher mentors were in direct collaboration with the researcher throughout the intervention. The teacher mentors provided input into the strategies used with their mentees and submitted bi-weekly reports to the researcher documenting their progress with mentees at every stage of the action research. The involvement of teachers, students, and researcher mirror the collaborative aspects of participatory action research, which Stringer (2007) described as democratic.

Third, the concept of systems thinking was evident and supports the assertion of Aronson (1996) who posits that for organizations to change, members must have broad perspectives of issues affecting the system. In this study, building relationships between teacher and student yielded deeper understanding of students' academic needs. The answers to the central research question regarding how a structured mentoring program can lead to an increase in enrollment of African-American males in advanced mathematics and science courses were best understood by a collaborative effort involving the key stakeholders.

Literature on the discourse of low achievement of African-American males lists several contributing factors categorized as individual factors, parental factors, and in school factors. Although the full extent of the various factors was not investigated, some of the findings were consistent with the literature reviewed regarding the assumptions teachers hold about the academic performance of African-American males. The survey on teacher perception indicated that 42.11% of teachers think some African-American males exhibit an 'I don't care' attitude, and another 26.32% indicated performance in class should be the only determining factor in placing students in advanced placement courses. Furthermore, 31.58% hold positive views about African-American males contrary to that of teachers who are of the perception that African-American males do not care. The 31.5% of teachers surveyed indicated some teachers hold low expectations of African-American male students. The teachers that hold negative views confirmed the assertion made by White (2009) who commented that teacher attitudes and expectations could impact student achievement. Specifically, the teachers' lower expectation of the student is based on the current performance of the student rather than on the students' potential to perform. Teachers must look for other ways to assess students to identify potentially talented students. The dialogue between mentor and mentee provides a suitable opportunity for reflection to evaluate the student mentee's abilities and needs.

This action research study's findings indicated a lack of parental involvement, societal, and in-school factors are barriers to African-American male students' academic achievement. These findings are consistent with the literature on these issues. The literature documented parents' academic expectations of African-American males compared to females diminish as they move on to higher levels of school (Graves, 2010); societal stereotypes seldom portray African-American males as accomplished scientist and mathematicians (Young, 2009); and there is a need for counselors to guide and mentor African-American males to enroll in college preparatory courses (Palmer et al., 2010).

Empirical studies of mentoring African-American males in high school to academic success, specifically in mathematics and science, are scanty in the literature. However, literature presented by the Quality Education for Minorities (QEM, 2010) mentioned earlier documents that mentoring minority males at a local high school is one strategy by which to increase their chances of enrollment in science, technology, engineering and mathematics courses. This latter documentation agrees with the findings of successful strategies unearthed during the mentoring intervention for this study. The Benjamin E. Mays Institute (BEMI) mentoring program conducted by Gordon et al. (2009), in which mentored middle school students were found to score higher GPA compared to those who were not mentored, confirmed that mentoring yields positive academic outcome.

Finally, students must enroll in a mathematics course-taking pathway that ensures enrollment in advanced mathematics and science courses to become eligible to enroll in college level courses. This study revealed nine of the 12 participating student mentees stated they would enroll in more advanced sections of mathematics. Eight of the nine students were enrolled in geometry (ninth and tenth-graders) and one was enrolled in algebra 2 (tenth-grader) indicating these African-American males are following the desired mathematics pathway that could eventually lead to enrolling in advanced mathematics and science courses. For example, ninth-graders taking geometry will proceed to enroll in Algebra 2 next school year (2014-2015), and tenth-graders enrolled in Algebra 2 will enroll in Pre-Calculus. This finding supports the assertion by Noble and Morton (2012) that students who enroll in advanced mathematics in previous years (e.g., pre-calculus) have a better chance of enrolling in future advanced sections of mathematics (calculus) before graduation.

Limitations

The study participants included male African-American students at a specific public high school; therefore, the findings may not be generalizable to all male African-American students of similar age in other high schools. Furthermore, these findings may not apply to black male students from other national origins. In addition, the mentoring intervention lasted only a short period. Most studies in the research literature on mentoring are conducted over longer periods of time and are longitudinal in nature.

Despite the short duration of time, the action research provided valuable insights into the effects of strategies to increase the enrollment of African-American males in advanced mathematics and science courses. The criteria for participation of African-American males did not include the socio-economic background of the students. For instance, whether the African-American males came from foster homes, single-family homes, or from homes with both parents was not considered. What was important in the choice of participants was the ability for student participants to remain committed throughout the intervention.

Participatory action research is defined by Stringer (2007) as action research in which participants are included in all aspects of the research design including planning, methodology, data collection, and interpretation of the results. Due to the limited time of the implementation of the action research, lasting only 20 sequential hours, collaboration with study participants and researcher was limited to development of the biweekly progress reports that contained strategies guiding the mentor-mentee interaction, feedback provided to the researcher every two weeks, and frequent dialogue with participants.

Implication of the Findings for Practice

The effects of strategies to increase the enrollment of male African-American high school students at a public high school in mathematics and science courses provide a viable approach to many of the deficit-focused research in the literature regarding the low academic performance of the targeted sub group of students. Although the study was confined to a small representative group of the African-American male population, the effects of strategies such as extra academic help, motivation, accountability, and clarifying concepts are tools educational practitioners can apply in the science and mathematics education of male minority high school students.

The study will contribute to the research knowledge base in the field of education in that it will further the understanding of how mentoring as an intervention can be structured to yield successful outcomes when educating African-American male students in STEM-related disciplines. The study has practical implications in disaggregating the data on other sub-group performances in mathematics and science, thereby causing Model 11 behaviors to resonate with all stakeholders in the organization pertaining to the unique needs of various sub-groups.

Recommendations for Further Research

Action research is cyclical in nature involving four basic steps: diagnosing, planning action, taking action, and evaluating action (Coughlan & Brannick, 2009). The cyclical nature of the study included four steps. First, the issue of low enrollment of African-American male high school students in advanced mathematics and science courses at a public high school was diagnosed. Second, planning of action to find solutions to the issue occurred in collaboration with key stakeholders. Third, action was taken via implementation of a mentoring program (the intervention). Lastly, the action taken was evaluated in the analyses of the findings. Going forward, it is recommended practitioners continue a second phase of the cycle in which to investigate ways to mitigate some of the challenges encountered in the intervention. For example, time management and the ability of teacher mentors to set a fixed schedule with their mentees was one challenge. Another challenge was finding ways to keep student mentees focused.

Practitioners should consider these issues in the next cycle of the action research.

Conclusion

Central to the action research study was an effort to determine how a mentoring program can be structured to effectively implement and yield successful outcomes for increased enrollment of African-American males in advanced sections of mathematics and sciences courses. To achieve this goal, the researcher investigated: (a) the attitudes African-American male high school aged students hold toward mathematics and science, (b) teacher perceptions and expectations about the enrollment of African-American males in mathematics and science courses, (c) elements of a structured mentoring program suitable for teachers, (d) and the impact of a school-based mentoring program.

Contrary to deficit-focused research on the achievement of African-American males in STEM related disciplines; African-American males were identified as having positive attitudes towards mathematics and science. The findings of the study indicated African-American males show positive attitudes towards mathematics and science evidenced by an average rating of 4.17 in the attitudinal survey.

When African-American males performed academically below expectation, teachers attributed the causes as being due to: (a) unfamiliarity with the gains in science and mathematics, (b) negative peer pressure, (c) lack of parental involvement, (d) teacher stereotypes and biases, and (e) lacking support of other stakeholders such as counselors.

A structured mentoring program must have important elements or criteria that serve as a blueprint for practitioners who are interested in assuming the role of a mentor. The findings indicated teachers as mentors must demonstrate: (a) effective time management, (b) the ability to set a fixed schedule with mentee, (c) the ability to provide academic support, (d) the ability to cater to mentee's specific needs, and (e) the ability to reflect on the mentee's classroom experiences as well as reflect on the mentor/mentee interactions.

Finally, mentoring as an intervention produces positive outcomes. The findings from the interviews with both mentees and mentors indicated a school-based mentoring program designed to enhance the enrollment of African-American males in advanced sections of mathematics and science courses should provide academic support as well as an opportunity to monitor and guide the progress of mentees throughout their high school experience.

REFERENCES

Anderson, K. (2008). Mentoring and standardized achievement of African-American males in the elementary and middle grades. *Middle Grades Research Journal, 2*(1), 49-72. Retrieved from people.uncw.edu/andersonk/Articles/Anderson_ mentoring.pdf

Argyris, C., & Schon, D. (2009). *Organizational learning II. Theory, method, and practice* (2nd ed.). Boston, MA: Addison-Wesley.

Aronson, D. (1996). *Overview of systems thinking.* Retrieved from http://resources21.org/cl/files/project264_5674/OverviewSTarticle.pdf

Barton, P. (2003). *Parsing the achievement gap. Baseline for tracking progress.* [Policy Information Report]. Retrieved from http://files.eric.ed.gov/fulltext/ ED482932.pdf

Battey, D. (2013). Good mathematics teaching for students of color and those in poverty: The importance of relational interactions within instruction. *Educational Studies in Mathematics, 82*(1), 125-144. doi:10.1007/s10649-012-9412-z

Bell, E. (2010). *Educating African-American males. Understanding Black males.* Retrieved from http://files.eric.ed.gov/fulltext/ED514552.pdf

Black, D. S., Grenard, J. L., Sussman, S., & Rohrbach, L. A. (2010). The influence of school-based natural mentoring relationships on school attachment and subsequent adolescent risk behaviors. *Health Education Research, 25*(5), 892– 902. doi:0.1093/her/cyq040

Coughlan, D., & Brannick, T. (2009). *Doing action research in your own organization* (3rd ed.). Thousand Oaks, CA: Sage.

Ford, D. Y., & Kea, C. D. (2009). Creating culturally responsive instruction: For students' and teachers' sake. *Focus on Exceptional Children, 41*(9), 82.

Fordham, S., & Ogbu, J. (1986). African American students' school success: Coping with the burden of acting White. *The Urban Review, 18*(3), 176-203.

Gall, M. D., Gall, J. P., & Borg, W. R. (2009). *Educational research: An introduction* (8th ed.). Upper Saddle River, NJ: Pearson.

Garrow, G., & Kaggwa, E. (2012). *Providing solutions for Black male achievement: Partnerships and mentoring.* Retrieved from http://files.eric.ed.gov/fulltext/ ED539625.pdf

Gordon D. M., Iwamoto, D., Ward, N., Potts, R., & Boyd E. (2009). Mentoring urban Black middle-school male students: Implications for academic achievement. *Negro Education, 78*(3), 277–289.

Graham, S., Taylor, A., & Hurdley, C. (1988). Exploring achievement values among ethnic minority early adolescents. *Journal of Educational Psychology, 90*(4), 606620. doi:10.1037/0022-0663.90.4.606

Graves, S. (2010). Are we neglecting African-American males: Parental involvement differences between African-American males and females during elementary school? *Journal of African American Studies, 14*(2), 263-276. doi:10.1007/s12111-0089065-2

Griffin, B. W. (2002). Academic disidentification, race, and high school dropouts. *High School Journal, 85*(4), 71-81. doi:10.1353/hsj.2002.0008

Griffin, K., & Allen, W. (2006). Mo' money, mo' problems? High-achieving Black high school students' experiences with resources, racial climate, and resilience. *The Journal of Negro Education, 75*(3), 478-494.

Herr, K., & Anderson, G. L. (2005). *The action research dissertation: A guide for students and faculty*. Thousand Oak, CA: Sage.

Herrera, C., Grossman, J., Kauh, T. J., & McMaken, J. (2011). Mentoring in schools: An impact study of Big Brothers Big Sisters school-based mentoring. *Child Development, 82*(1), 346-361. doi:10.1111/j.1467-8624.2010.01559.x

Jenkins H. L. (1976). *Causes of low enrollment of Black students in upper-level science courses* (Master's thesis). Retrieved from http://digitalcommons.unf.edu/cgi/viewcontent.cgi?article=1006&context=etd

Kober, N. (2001). *It takes more than testing: Closing the achievement gap*. [A report of the center on education policy]. Washington, DC: Center on Educational Policy.

Madyun, N. H. (2011). Connecting social disorganization theory to African-American outcomes to explain the achievement gap. *The Journal of Educational Foundations, 25*(3), 21-35.

McMillan, J. (2011). *Educational research. Fundamentals for the consumer* (6th ed.). Boston, MA: Pearson.

Mentee. (2014). *What is a mentee?* Retrieved from http://mentorscout.com/about/ mentor.cfm

Mentor. (n.d.). In *Merriam-Webster's online dictionary* (11th ed.). Retrieved from www.merriam-webster.com/thesaurus/mentors

Museus, S. D., Palmer, R. T., Davis, R. J., & Maramba, D. C. (2011). Special issue: Racial and ethnic minority students' success in STEM education. *ASHE Higher Education Report 36*(6), 1-140.

National Center for Education Statistics. (2005). *Status and trends in the education of racial and ethnic minorities*. Retrieved from http://nces.ed.gov/pubs2007/ minority trends/tables/table_4b.asp?referrer=report

Noble, R., & Morton, C. (2013). African Americans and mathematics outcomes on national assessment of educational progress: Parental and individual influences. *Journal of Child & Family Studies, 22*(1), 30-37. doi:10.1007/s10826-012- 9640-y

Ogbu, J. (1994). Racial stratification and education in the United States:

Why inequality persists. *The Teachers College Record, 96*(2), 264-298.

Orthner, D., Jones-Sanpei, H., & Williamson, S. (2004). The resilience and strengths of low-income families. *Family Relations, 53(2),* 159-167. doi:10.1111/j.00222445.2004.00006.x

Osborne, J. W. (1999). Unraveling underachievement among African-American boys from an identification with academics perspective. *The Journal of Negro Education, 68*(4), 555-565.

Palmer T. R., Davis R. J., Moore J. L., & Hilton, A. A. (2010). A nation at risk: Increasing college participation and persistence among African-American males to stimulate U.S. global competitiveness. *Journal of African-American males in Education. 1*(2), 105-124.

Poliakoff, A. (2006). Closing the achievement gap. An Overview, *Infobrief, 44.* Retrieved from http://intranet.niacc.edu/pres_copy(1)/ILC/Closing%20the%20Gap%20%20An%20Overview.pdf

Quality Education for Minorities, (2010). *Regional workshops on the recruitment and retention of minority males in STEM disciplines at minority-serving institutions.* Washington, DC. Retrieved from http://www.qem.org/QEM_MinorityMalesinSTEMInitiative.htm

Ryzin, M. (2010). Secondary school advisors as mentors and secondary attachment figures. *Journal of Community Psychology, 38*(2), 131-154. doi:10.1002/jcop.20356

Sciarra, D. T. (2010). Predictive factors in intensive math course-taking in high school. *Professional School Counseling, 13*(3), 196-207. doi:0.5330/PSC.n.2010-13.196

Shenton, A. (2004). Strategies for ensuring trustworthiness in qualitative research projects. *Education for Information, 22*(2004), 63-75. Retrieved from http://www.angelfire.com/theforce/shu_cohort_viii/images/Trustworthypaper.pdf

Steele, C. M. (2003). Race and the schooling of Black Americans. In S. Plous (Ed.), *Understanding prejudice and discrimination* (pp. 98-107). New York, NY: McGraw-Hill.

Stringer, E. T. (2007). *Action research.* Thousand Oaks, CA: Sage.

Tierney, J. P., & Grossman, J. B. (2000*). Making a difference: An impact study of big brothers and sisters.* Philadelphia, PA: Public/Private Ventures.

Toldson, I. A. (2008). *Breaking barriers: Plotting the path to academic success for school-age African-American males.* Washington, DC: Congressional Black Caucus Foundation, Inc.

Tucker, C., Dixon, A., & Griddine, K. (2010). Academically successful African American male urban high school students' experiences of mattering to others at school. *Professional School Counseling, 14*(2), 135-145.

Washington, J. (2011, October 23). STEM education and jobs: Declining numbers of Blacks seen in math, science. *Huffington Post.* Retrieved from http://www.huffingtonpost.com/2011/10/24/stem-education-and-jobsd_n_1028998.html

West-Olatunji, C., Shure, L., Garrett, M. T., Conwell, W., Rivera, E. T. (2011). Rite of passage programs as effective tools for fostering resilience among low-income African American male adolescents. *Journal of Humanistic Counseling, Education & Development, 47*(2), 131-143. doi:10.1002/j.2161-1939.2008.tb00053.x

Western Association of Schools & Colleges. (2010). A report prepared for public school A by the 2010 visiting accreditation team representing the *Western Association of Schools & Colleges.* Retrieved from http://www.csustan.edu/wasc

White, H. E. (2009). Increasing the achievement of African-American males. *Department of Research, Evaluation, and Assessment, 3.* Retrieved from http://www. vbschools.com/accountability/research_briefs/aamalebrieffinalamar ch.pdf

Williams, P. (2008). *Emergent themes.* Retrieved from http://knowledge.sagepub. com/view/research/n129.xml

Young J. F. (2009). *African American success foundation: A study of academically high achieving economically challenged African American young men* (Doctoral dissertation). Available from ProQuest dissertations and Theses database. (UMI No. 3368392)

APPENDICES

APPENDIX A

Biweekly Progress Report

Study Topic: Evaluating Strategies to Increase the Enrollment of African-American Male High School Students in Advanced Mathematics and Science Courses

Mentor's Name:

_____

Mentee's Name(s):

_____

Strategies used with mentee (check all that apply)

___Helped with homework

___Discussed study skills and monitored mentee's application of study skills

___Assigned mentee practice problems in math & science (mentor as tutor)

___Mentor recommended after school tutoring for mentee, and evaluated mentee's progress in the after-school tutoring program (how is mentee doing? Mentee can show mentor al log of afterschool tutoring attendance)

___Collaborated with science and or mentee's teacher (can mentee retake a test?/Monitor assigned chapter's mentee should study/any short or long term projects? Tell mentee's math & science teacher that you are mentee's mentor seeking ways to prepare mentee to enroll in advanced mathematics and science courses)

___Gave mentee at least two web sites as enrichment exercise to reinforce math and science concepts (to manage this activity- perhaps you and mentee can discuss the usefulness of these web sites as study strategy).

___Contributions strategy - had mentee research the contributions of modern day African-American males in science, technology, engineering and mathematics (to manage this activity, mentee can write notes, which can be discussed with mentor).

___Discussed with mentee his career goals and how mathematics and science play a role in mentee's choice of career.

___Discussed the various fields /job opportunities in science and mathematics with mentee, and the salary paid for those jobs (manage this activity by providing at least five science-mathematics-related careers).

___Discussed the importance of taking advanced courses in mathematics & science with mentee (Perhaps to be college ready, etc.)

Comments (optional)

_____

APPENDIX B

Letter to Counselors

Dear Counselors,

Mr. David Macauley will be conducting an Action Research study at this school site. Mr. Macauley is a doctoral student in the school of education at Capella University, located in Minneapolis, Minnesota. Mr. Macauley's research supervisor is Dr. Yvonne Barnes (email address).

The purpose of the research is to evaluate the effects of strategies to increase the enrollment of African American males in advanced mathematics and science courses at your school site. Each participating student will be assigned a mentor (one of their consenting teachers), and they will be required to spend approximately 2-3 hours a week for a total of about 20 hours' duration of the entire study interacting with their mentors. In addition, they are required to take an online survey lasting no more than 20 minutes.

As a counselor with access to students' records, the researcher, Mr. Macauley would like your assistance in recruiting 10 to 15 African American male students in grades 9 and 10 to participate in the Action Research. Participating students must meet the following criteria: they must have a grade of at least a C in mathematics in their previous or current class, and must have scored at the basic or proficient level in mathematics in their most recent state standardized test. Please compile a list of all eligible African American male students per the above criteria. The compiled list will be collected within one week from this notification. The researcher will then ensure delivery of a recruitment letter to all the eligible student participants whose names appear on the list.

There are no benefits for the study, but the results will help other researchers. In appreciation of their time, participating students will receive a $10 gift card to Juice It Up.

The researcher has been granted permission to conduct this Action research by the assistant superintendent of educational services, Dr. Kedziora, and in addition received ethics clearance by Capella University's Institutional Review Board.

For all communication pertaining to this request, please contact Mr. Macauley by email / telephone numbers: (Listed)

Thank you.
Mr. Macauley

APPENDIX C

Letter to Students

Dear Student,

Mr. Macauley will do a study at your school. The reason for the study is to find ways to increase the enrollment of African American male students in advanced mathematics and science courses in your school. Your counselor has identified you as meeting the requirement for participation; this means that you have a grade of C in mathematics in your previous or current class, and you scored at the basic or proficient level in mathematics in your most recent state standardized test score.

As a participant of this study, one of your teachers will be assigned as your mentor. You will be required to spend at least 2-3 hours a week (beyond normal school time) with your mentor (teacher) for a total of about 20 hours. Please follow carefully the instructions of your mentor always. You will also take an online survey lasting no more than 20 minutes.

There are no benefits to you for this study, but the results will help other researchers. In appreciation of your time, you will receive a $10 gift card to Juice It Up.

You can let Mr. Macauley know if you are interested immediately after reading this letter, or if you need some time, say within a week you can inform one of your teachers, who will then notify me by email of your decision to participate or not.

Mr. Macauley's room number is (##), and you can stop by within one week after reading this letter to let him know your decision. You can also reach him at (telephone number) or you can email him directly at (email address).

Mr. Macauley has received permission form the assistant superintendent, Dr. Kedziora, and committee members of Capella University to do this action research.

Please do your best to contact Mr. Macauley within the time frame mentioned above.

Thank you.

APPENDIX D

Parental Permission Form

**Study Title: Evaluating the Effects of Strategies to
Increase the Enrollment of African-American
males in Advanced Mathematics And Science.**

Researcher: David Macauley
Email and Telephone #:
Research Supervisor: Dr. Yvonne Barnes
Email and Telephone #:

Your child is invited to be part of a research
study. The researcher is a doctoral learner at Capella
University in the School of Education. This form
describes the study to help you decide if your child
should participate. This form will tell you what your
child will have to do during the study and the risks and
benefits of the study.

If you have any questions about or do not
understand something in this form, you should ask the
researcher. You should discuss your child's
participation with anyone you choose to better
understand this study and your options. Do not sign
this form unless the researcher has answered your
questions and you decide that you want your child to
be part of this study.

WHAT IS THIS STUDY ABOUT?

The researcher wants to learn about ways to prepare African American male students to enroll in advanced mathematics and science courses in their junior and senior years. If for any reason you do not wish to work with your assigned mentor, you may decline; another mentor will then be assigned to you.

WHY IS MY CHILD BEING ASKED TO BE IN THE STUDY?

Your child is invited to be in the study because he is:

- An African American male student
- Having a current mathematics grade of C or better, and scores at the basic or proficient level in the most recent California standardized tests.
- A freshman or sophomore in the 2013/2014 school year

All participants will be between the ages of 14 and 16.

What is my role as a parent if I give consent for my child to participate in this study?

As a parent, your role will be purely supportive throughout the study. Your assistance in making sure your child follows the instruction of his mentor will be appreciated. Keep in mind this research will help other researchers to unearth solutions to improving the academic performance of African American males in mathematics and science courses, thereby giving them a chance to enroll in advanced course sections.

HOW MANY PEOPLE WILL BE IN THIS STUDY?

About 10 to 15 students and 20 teachers will be in the study.

WHO IS PAYING FOR THIS STUDY?

The researcher is not receiving funds to conduct this study. The researcher is employed at (name of) school district, and is currently teaching at (name of) high school, but is not receiving funds to conduct this study. The researcher will not be paid for conducting the study.

WILL IT COST ANYTHING TO BE IN THIS STUDY?

You do not have to pay for your child to be in the study.

HOW LONG WILL MY CHILD BE IN THE STUDY?

If you decide to let your child be in this study and your child decides to be in the study and the researcher says your child can be in the study, your child's participation will last about 20 hours (this time includes one on one discussion with mentor only. Mentee is required to consistently work on his study goals and make progress.)

Your child will participate in the study at (name of) High School. One of his teachers will be his mentor, and check with him at least 2-3 hours a week. The mentor will monitor your son's progress in mathematics and science, and provide academic help when necessary. If for any reason your child does not want to work with the assigned mentor, he may decline and another, and another mentor will be assigned (the researcher will ensure mentees are comfortable with assigned mentors).

You do not need to transport your child anywhere. However, although it is not mandatory your child's mentor teacher may recommend that your child be enrolled in after school tutoring or stay at least 30 mins after school to review concepts with his assigned mentor teacher. Should the mentor teacher recommend after school help, you will be notified to make arrangements to pick up your child.

WHAT WILL HAPPEN TO MY CHILD DURING THIS STUDY?

If you decide to let your child be in this study and if you sign this form, your child will do the following things:

- Answer questions during an interview about the benefits of the mentoring program.
- Complete a survey about how they feel about mathematics and science. The survey will be conducted using school computers under the supervision / safety policies of the school district.
- Allow the researcher to look at your child's records, such as his grades in mathematics and science as well as his most recent California standardized test score.
- Follow all instructions/directions given by his mentor teacher.

Your child also must agree to participate in the study and sign an assent form (a form that your child signs giving his consent to participate in the study).

While your child is in the study, your child must:

- Follow the instructions given.
- Tell the researcher if he wants to stop being in the study at any time.

WILL MY CHILD BE RECORDED?

No, your child will not be recorded. The researcher will take notes during your child's interview. The written notes will be kept confidential for seven years, after which they will be destroyed.

WILL BEING IN THIS STUDY HELP ME OR MY CHILD?

Being in this study will not help you. However, it might provide insight to researchers interested in similar studies.

ARE THERE RISKS TO MY CHILD IF HE/SHE IS IN THIS STUDY?

No study is completely risk-free. However, we don't anticipate that your child will be harmed or distressed during this study. You may stop being in the study at any time if you become uncomfortable.

WILL I OR MY CHILD GET PAID?

You will not receive anything for being in the study. The researcher will however consider some rewards for your child, such as a $10 gift card to Juice It Up.

DOES MY CHILD HAVE TO BE IN THIS STUDY?

Your child's participation in this study is voluntary. You can decide not to have your child in the study. You can change your mind at any time. There will be no penalty to your child. If you want your child's participation to stop, tell the researcher.

WHO WILL USE AND SHARE INFORMATION ABOUT MY CHILD BEING IN THIS STUDY?

Any information your child provides in this study that could identify him, such as his name, age, or other personal information will be kept confidential. In any written reports or publications, no one will be able to identify your child.

The researcher will keep the information you and your child provides in a password protected computer and/or a locked file cabinet in the researcher's private office, and only the researcher, research supervisor and the researcher's dissertation committee members will be able to review this information.

Even if your child leaves the study early, the researcher may still be able to use your child's data. For example, the responses to the survey questions provided by your child will still be used in the study.

LIMITS OF PRIVACY (CONFIDENTIALITY)

Generally speaking, the researcher can assure you that he will keep everything you tell him or do for the study private. Yet there are times where the researcher cannot keep things private (confidential). The researcher cannot keep things private (confidential) when:

- The researcher finds out a child or vulnerable adult has been abused
- The researcher finds out that a person plans to hurt him or herself, such as commit suicide, or
- The researcher finds out a person plans to hurt someone else.

There are laws that require many professionals (teachers, educational staff, and/or administration) to take action if they think a person might harm themselves or another, or if a child or adult is being abused. There are guidelines researchers must follow to ensure all people within the study are treated with respect and kept safe. In most states, there is a government agency that must be informed if someone is being abused or plans to hurt themselves or another person. Please ask any questions you may have about this issue before agreeing to be in the study. It is important you do not feel betrayed if it turns out the researcher cannot keep some things private.

WHO CAN I TALK TO ABOUT THIS STUDY?

You can ask questions about the study at any time. You can call the researcher at any time if you have any concerns or complaints. You should call the researcher at the phone number listed on page 1 of this form if you have questions about the study procedures, study costs (if any), study payment (if any), or if your child gets hurt or sick during the study.
The Capella Research Integrity Office (RIO)

has been established to protect the rights and welfare of human research participants. Please contact us at (phone #), extension (XXX), for any of the following reasons:

- You have questions about your rights as a research participant.
- You wish to discuss problems or concerns.
- You have suggestions to improve the participant experience.
- You do not feel comfortable talking with the researcher.

You may contact the RIO without giving us your name. We may need to reveal information you provide to follow up if you report a problem or concern.

DO YOU WANT TO BE IN THIS STUDY?

I have read this form, and I have been able to ask questions about this study. The researcher has talked with me about this study. The researcher has answered all my questions. I voluntarily agree to allow my child to be in this study. I agree to allow the use and sharing of my child's study-related records as described above. By signing this form, I have not given up any of my legal rights. I will get a signed copy of this form for my records.

_____
Printed Name of Parent/Guardian

_____
Printed Name of Parent/Guardian

_____
Date

_____

Name of Child

    I attest the participant named above had enough time to consider this information, had an opportunity to ask questions, and voluntarily agreed to be in this study.

_____

Printed Name of Researcher

_____

Signature of Researcher

_____

Date

APPENDIX E

Consent Form – Ages 12-17

Study Title: Evaluating the Effects of Strategies to Increase the Enrollment of African American Males in Advanced Mathematics and Science.

Researcher: David Macauley
Email and Telephone #:
Research Supervisor: Dr. Yvonne Barnes
Email and Telephone #:

You are invited to be part of a research study. The researcher is a doctoral learner at Capella University in the School of education. The information in this form is provided to help you decide if you want to participate. The form describes what you will have to do during the study and the risks and benefits of the study.

If you have any questions about or do not understand something in this form, you should ask the researcher. Do not sign this form unless the researcher has answered your questions and you decide that you want to be part of this study.

WHAT IS THIS STUDY ABOUT?

The researcher wants to learn about how he can increase your chances of enrolling in advanced mathematics and science courses in your junior and senior years. The research topic is: Evaluating the effects of strategies to increase the enrollment of African American males in advanced mathematics and science courses.

Basically, participating African American male students will be assigned a mentor teacher who will give guidance and help students improve on their mathematics and science skills.

WHY AM I BEING ASKED TO BE IN THE STUDY?

You are invited to be in the study because you are:

- An African American male student
- You have a grade of at least a C in mathematics, and you scored at the basic or proficient level in your most recent California standards test.

All participants will be between the ages of 14-16 years. If you do not meet the description above, you are not able to be in the study.

HOW MANY PEOPLE WILL BE IN THIS STUDY?

About 10 -15 students and 20 teachers will be in this study.

WHO IS PAYING FOR THIS STUDY?

The researcher is not receiving funds to conduct this study.

WILL IT COST ANYTHING TO BE IN THIS STUDY?

Your parent/guardian does not have to pay to be in the study.

WHAT WILL HAPPEN DURING THIS STUDY?

If you decide to be in this study and if you sign this form, you will do the following things:

- Give personal information about yourself, such as your age, gender, and mathematics and science grades.
- Answer questions during an interview about your experiences and benefits of the mentor program or a chance to say what you did not like about the program.
- Complete a survey about your attitude or the way you feel about mathematics and science.
- Allow a researcher to look at your records, such as your grades in science, mathematics, and your California standardized test scores.
- Maintain a positive relationship with your mentor teacher

While you are in the study, you will be expected to:

- Follow the instructions you are given.
- Tell the researcher if you want to stop being in the study at any time.

WILL I BE RECORDED?

No, you will not be recorded. The researcher will take notes during interviews.

WILL BEING IN THIS STUDY HELP ME?

Being in this study will not help you. However,

it might provide insight to researchers interested in similar studies.

ARE THERE RISKS TO ME IF I AM IN THIS STUDY?

No study is completely risk-free. However, we don't anticipate that you will be harmed or distressed during this study. You may stop being in the study at any time if you become uncomfortable.

WILL I GET PAID?

If you participate, you will receive a $10 gift card to Juice It Up.

DO I HAVE TO BE IN THIS STUDY?

Your participation in this study is voluntary. You can decide not to be in the study and you can change your mind about being in the study at any time. There will be no penalty to you. If you want to stop being in the study, tell the researcher.

Your parent(s)/guardian(s) have also said that you may participate in this study.

The researcher can remove you from the study at any time. This could happen if:

- The researcher believes it is best for you to stop being in the study.
- You do not follow directions about the study.
- You no longer meet the inclusion criteria to participate

WHO WILL USE AND SHARE INFORMATION ABOUT MY BEING IN THIS STUDY?

Any information you provide in this study that could identify you such as your name, age, or other personal information will be kept confidential. The researcher's computer is password protected, also in any written reports or publications; no one will be able to identify you.

The researcher will keep the information you provide in a password protected computer and a locked file cabinet in his private office, and Capella University's data base, and only the researcher, research supervisor, and the researcher's committee members will be able to review this information.

There will be no tape recordings.

Even if you leave the study early, the researcher may still be able to use your data. For example, your responses to the survey you will take earlier in the study will be used.

Limits of Privacy (Confidentiality)

Generally speaking, the researcher can assure you that he will keep everything you tell him or do for the study private. Yet there are times where the researcher cannot keep things private (confidential). The researcher cannot keep things private (confidential) when:

- The researcher finds out that a child or vulnerable adult has been abused
- The researcher finds out that a person plans to

hurt him or herself, such as commit suicide, or
- The researcher finds out that a person plans to hurt someone else.

There are laws that require many professionals to take action if they think a person might harm themselves or another, or if a child or adult is being abused. In addition, there are guidelines that researchers must follow to make sure all people are treated with respect and kept safe. In most states, there is a government agency that must be told if someone is being abused or plans to hurt themselves or another person. Please ask any questions you may have about this issue before agreeing to be in the study. It is important that you do not feel betrayed if it turns out that the researcher cannot keep some things private.

WHO CAN I TALK TO ABOUT THIS STUDY?

You can ask questions about the study at any time. You can call the researcher at any time if you have any concerns or complaints. You should call the researcher at the phone number listed on page 1 of this form if you have questions about the study procedures, or if you get hurt or sick during the study.

The Capella Research Integrity Office (RIO) has been established to protect the rights and welfare of human research participants. Please contact us at (phone ##), for any of the following reasons:

- You have questions about your rights as a research participant.
- You wish to discuss problems or concerns.
- You have suggestions to improve the participant experience.

- You do not feel comfortable talking with the researcher.

You may contact the RIO without giving us your name. We may need to reveal information you provide to follow up if you report a problem or concern.

DO YOU WANT TO BE IN THIS STUDY?

I have read this form, and I have been able to ask questions about this study. The researcher has talked with me about this study. The researcher has answered all my questions. I voluntarily agree to be in this study. I agree to allow the use and sharing of my study-related records as described above.

By signing this form, I have not given up any of my legal rights as a research participant. I will get a signed copy of this consent form for my records.

_____
Printed Name of Participant
_____
Signature of Participant
_____
Date

I attest the participant named above had enough time to consider this information, had an opportunity to ask questions, and voluntarily agreed to be in this study.

_____
Printed Name of Researcher
_____
Signature of Researcher
_____

Date

DO YOU WISH TO BE AUDIO/VIDEOTAPED IN THIS STUDY? (Leave blank if you do not agree)

     I voluntarily agree to let the researcher audiotape me for this study. I agree to allow the use of my recordings as described in this form.

_____

Printed Name of Participant

_____

Signature of Participant

_____

Date

Capella IRB Approval

APPENDIX F

Informed Consent Form (Adult/Teachers)

Study Title: Evaluating the Effects of Strategies to Increase the Enrollment of African American Males in Advanced Mathematics and Science: An Action Research.

Researcher: David Macauley
Email and Telephone #:
Research Supervisor: Dr. Yvonne Barnes
Email and Telephone #:

You are invited to be part of a research study. The researcher is a doctoral learner at Capella University in the School of education. The information in this form is provided to help you decide if you want to participate. The form describes what you will have to do during the study and the risks and benefits of the study.

If you have any questions about or do not understand something in this form, you should ask the researcher. Do not sign this form unless the researcher has answered your questions and you decide that you want to be part of this study.

WHAT IS THIS STUDY ABOUT?

The researcher wants to learn about the effects of strategies to increase the enrollment of African

American males in advanced mathematics and science courses via a mentoring program. Participating students will be assigned a mentor teacher, who will guide them into improving their skills in mathematics and science. The researcher wants to find if the mentoring intervention will increase the likelihood that more African American males will enroll in advanced courses in mathematics and science in their junior and senior years.

WHY AM I BEING ASKED TO BE IN THE STUDY?

You are invited to be in the study because you are:

- A teacher in the school, who is deemed capable of being a positive influence in the achievement of the students, you do not need to be a mathematics or science teacher to participate in the study.

Method of Assignment

- Once you have indicated consent to participate, you will be randomly assigned a mentee, however mentees may choose to accept or decline the match for any reason

Your Role as a Mentor

As a mentor your role will be:

- Helping with classwork/homework
- Helping with projects (during lunch or after school)
- Discussion about being successful in school
- Discussion about choosing careers in science, technology, engineering and mathematics

- Provide information about ways students can participate in mathematics and science enrichment programs in the community, like science and math workshops for teens.
A training session for all mentors will be conducted in the library prior to the commencement

The Nature of Tutoring

You may choose to offer tutoring help via three options:

- Offer tutoring help to mentee directly before school, during lunch, or after school if you are knowledgeable in mathematics and science.
- Recommend that mentee enroll in after school tutoring with mentor holding student accountable by checking attendance logs (parental permission will be required for student to stay after school)
- Work in partnership with mentee's mathematics, and science teachers to monitor mentee's progress, and ensure that teachers clarify concepts with mentee as needed.

All participants will be between the ages 14-16 years old for the students, and 21-65 years old for the teachers. If you do not meet the description above, you are not able to be in the study.

HOW MANY PEOPLE WILL BE IN THIS STUDY?

About 10-15 students, and 20 teachers will participate in this study.

WHO IS PAYING FOR THIS STUDY?

The researcher is not receiving funds to conduct this study.

WILL IT COST ANYTHING TO BE IN THIS STUDY?

You do not have to pay to be in the study.

HOW LONG WILL I BE IN THE STUDY?

If you decide to be in this study, your participation will last about 20 hours if you serve as a mentor. If you are invited to take a survey only, you will not spend more than 20 minutes taking the survey. The study will be conducted at your school site.

WHAT WILL HAPPEN DURING THIS STUDY?

If you decide to be in this study and if you sign this form, you will do the following things:

- Give personal information about yourself, such as your gender, years of teaching experience, and education level.
- Answer questions during an interview about your evaluation of the mentoring program (intervention)
- Complete a survey about teacher perception of African American male students
- Submit a bi-weekly progress report to the researcher, as way of tracking the progress of your assigned mentee (s)

While you are in the study, you will be expected to:

- Follow the instructions you are given.
- Tell the researcher if you want to stop being in the study at any time.

WILL I BE RECORDED?

No, you will not be recorded.

WILL BEING IN THIS STUDY HELP ME?

Being in this study will not help you. However, it might provide insight to researchers interested in similar studies.

ARE THERE RISKS TO ME IF I AM IN THIS STUDY?

No study is completely risk-free. However, we don't anticipate that you will be harmed or distressed during this study. You may stop being in the study at any time if you become uncomfortable.

WILL I GET PAID?

If you participate, you will receive a $20 gift card to Starbucks.

DO I HAVE TO BE IN THIS STUDY?

Your participation in this study is voluntary. You can decide not to be in the study and you can change your mind about being in the study at any time. There will be no penalty to you. If you want to stop being in the study, tell the researcher.

The researcher can remove you from the study at any time. This could happen if:

- The researcher believes it is best for you to stop being in the study.
- You do not follow directions about the study.
- You no longer meet the inclusion criteria to participate.

WHO WILL USE AND SHARE INFORMATION ABOUT MY BEING IN THIS STUDY?

Any information you provide in this study that could identify you such as your name, age, or other personal information will be kept confidential. In any written reports or publications, no one will be able to identify you.

The researcher will keep the information you provide in a password protected computer and locked file cabinet in the researcher's private office, and on Capella University's data base. Only the researcher, research supervisor, and the researcher's committee members will be able to review this information.

Even if you leave the study early, the researcher may still be able to use your data. Your responses to the survey, which you will take early in the study will be used.

LIMITS OF PRIVACY (CONFIDENTIALITY)

Generally speaking, the researcher can assure you that he will keep everything you tell him/her or do for the study private. Yet there are times where the researcher cannot keep things private (confidential). The researcher cannot keep things private (confidential) when:

- The researcher finds out that a child or vulnerable adult has been abused
- The researcher finds out that that a person plans to hurt him or herself, such as commit suicide,
- The researcher finds out that a person plans to hurt someone else,

There are laws that require many professionals to take action if they think a person might harm themselves or another, or if a child or adult is being abused. In addition, there are guidelines that researchers must follow to make sure all people are treated with respect and kept safe. In most states, there is a government agency that must be told if someone is being abused or plans to hurt themselves or another person. Please ask any questions you may have about this issue before agreeing to be in the study. It is important that you do not feel betrayed if it turns out that the researcher cannot keep some things private.

WHO CAN I TALK TO ABOUT THIS STUDY?

You can ask questions about the study at any time. You can call the researcher if you have any concerns or complaints. You should call the researcher at the phone number listed on page 1 of this form if you have questions about the study procedures, study costs (if any), study payment (if any), or if you get hurt or sick during the study.

The Capella Research Integrity Office (RIO) has been established to protect the rights and welfare of human research participants. Please contact us at (phone #), for any of the following reasons:

- You have questions about your rights as a research participant.
- You wish to discuss problems or concerns.
- You have suggestions to improve the participant experience.
- You do not feel comfortable talking with the researcher.

You may contact the RIO without giving us your name. We may need to reveal information you provide to follow up if you report a problem or concern.

INDEX

CURRICULUM VITAE

David Raymond. O. Macauley, Ed.D.
Moreno Valley, CA 92557
(951) 413-4633 / davidrmacauley@gmail.com

TEACHING PHILOSOPHY

My philosophy of teaching has evolved over 20 years of teaching. I believe all students can learn regardless of their circumstances. What is most profound as I reflect on my interaction with students is the ability to determine the potential and promise of students rather than focusing on their deficits. To discover the potential of my students I always give them an opportunity to discover their intellectual capacity by engaging them in ways that allow them to think critically as they provide answers to real-life problems.

Asking my students compelling questions that ultimately spark curiosity results in advancement of critical thinking skills. I also believe for students to succeed; I must have knowledge of all the variables that may be affecting each student's potential to perform. In other words, the affective domain of each child is just as important as their cognitive and intellectual domain. I am also of the firm belief that character development is important to the success of students from kindergarten through 12th grade. I have high expectations for all students; therefore, all students must master fundamental character traits for life-long success. For example, it is important students understand the need for self-discipline, self-control, respect for self and others, building relationships with others, and collaborating amicably in a team effort to attain excellence.

PROFESSIONAL TEACHING EXPERIENCE

2017 – Present, Adjunct Professor
University of California, Riverside Ext., Riverside, CA

- Botany for Educators. Topics include: Plant Structure and Function, Plant Classification and Systematics, Plant Physiology, Genetics and Ecology; geared towards preparation for secondary teaching credential in Life Science
- Access and Equity in Science, Technology, Engineering and Mathematics (STEM) Education (Online Instruction). Topics include: Introduction to STEM Equity, Culturally Relevant STEM Education, Technology and STEM Teachers, Gender Equity in STEM Education, and STEM Best Practices

2006 – present, Multi-level Biology Teacher
Moreno Valley Unified School District, CA

1997 – 2006, Middle School Science Teacher
Los Angeles Unified School District
Los Angeles, CA

- Contributed to the design of inquiry and enrichment activities aligned with California State Standards for 7th grade Life Science students; teaching five classes, with a maximum of 36 students per class

1994 – 1997, Special Education Instructor
New Citizens Non-Public School, Los Angeles, CA

- Developed curriculum tailored to needs of students in grades 7 and 8 per Individualized Education Plan (IED); Class was self-contained with a maximum of 10 students daily

1992 – 1994, Science and Mathematics Teacher, Middle-School West Angeles Christian Academy Los Angeles, CA

- Taught General science and Mathematics using the A Beka curriculum; educational approach of the A Beka curriculum is based on biblical principles tied to subjects with biblical reference
- Class sizes consisted of no more than two sets of 20 students per class

PROFESSIONAL LEADERSHIP EXPERIENCE

2013 – Present, Member, Leadership Team, Valley View High School, Moreno Valley, CA

- Meet with other team members monthly to discuss school-wide issues pertaining to student achievement

2013 – Present, Member, School Site Council, Valley View High School, Moreno Valley, CA

- Meet with team members monthly for decisions, and approvals regarding allocation of fiscal resources, particularly Title 1 funds

LEADERSHIP EXPERIENCE

Educational Leadership

- Collaborate with the leadership team to implement the school plan leading to student achievement at Valley View High, Moreno Valley Unified School District, Moreno Valley, CA
- Collaborate with the Valley View high school site council members to approve budgets and Title 1 funds

to fund various needs such as technology, and other resources resulting in student achievement

- 2008, 2010, 2014, Led three summer study abroad trips to England, France, and Italy (2008), Italy and France (2010), Spain, and Greece (2014) for more than 90 students in three years resulting in exposure to international cultures for high school students from Moreno Valley, Perris, and Riverside, CA.
- 2013 – present, Symposium lead coordinator for African-American sub-group. The symposium is titled "No limits No Excuses" with goal to promote a school culture of respect and high expectations for all students. Number of attendees have increased from 50 to 400 students culminating in reduced suspension rate as well as contributing to a 5% increase in the graduation rate of A-A students. These results are compared to previous suspension, and graduation data when symposia weren't held.
- 2009 – 2015, Co-Advisor Eagle Scholars; supervised student leadership of Eagle Scholars, responsible for screening, invitation, and processing applications to monitor and mentor incoming freshmen at Valley View high school so they stay in good academic standing with ultimate preparation for membership in National Honor Society in their junior year.

EDUCATION

- 2014, Doctorate in Education, Educational Leadership and Management, Capella University, Minneapolis, MN. Courses: Foundations of Educational Leadership and Management, Leadership Through Personal and Professional Development, Creating a Culture of Learning, Data Informed Decision Making for Educational Leaders, Leading and Managing Change, and Dissertation Research

- 2004, Master of Arts in Education, Multi-Cultural Education, California State University, Dominguez Hills, CA. Courses: Socio Cultural Issues in Education, Evaluation & Program Monitor in Education, Teaching English Speakers Other Language, Seminar-Issues in Education, Seminar- Mexican-American & Hispanic Education, and Education of Mexican-American & Hispanic Students

- 1990, Bachelor of Science (Joint Honors), Zoology and Botany, Fourah Bay College, Sierra Leone, West Africa. Courses: Principles of Biology, Chemistry, Intro. to Organic Chemistry, Computer Applications for Science, Statistics & Probability, General Physics, Plant Physiology, Human Physiology, Cell Biology, Ecology, Genetics, Cell & Genetics Laboratory, Marine Biology, Comparative Vertebrate Biology & Microbiology

TRAINING CERTIFICATIONS

- 2015, Preliminary Administrative Services Credential, Redlands University, CA
- Moreno Valley Leadership Academy Consortium, Moreno Valley, CA
- 2001, Single Subject Teaching Credential in Biology and Geo Sciences /Cross Cultural Language and Acquisition (CLAD), California State University, Dominguez Hills, CA

WORKSHOPS AND SEMINARS

- 2015, Presenter, *Strategies to increase the enrollment of AA high school males in advanced mathematics and science courses*, California Association of African American Superintendents and Administrators

- 2015, Contributor, Common Core Curriculum and Standards Planning for High School Students
- 2007, Participant, Sheltered Instruction Observation Protocol for English Language Learners (SIOP)

PUBLICATIONS

Macauley, D. (2016). *Increasing Enrollment of African-American Males in Advanced High School STEM Courses: Increasing Enrollment of African American Males in High School Advanced Math & Science Classes.* Virginia Beach / Richmond, VA: DBC Publishing.

Macauley, D. (2014). *Increasing the Enrollment of African-American Males in Advanced Mathematics and Science Courses in High School.* Dissertation # 3644281; ProQuest document ID #: 1626021004.

COMMUNITY INVOLVEMENT / ENTREPRENEURSHIP

2007 – Present, Founder/Co-Owner
Better Grades Now Tutoring Services
www.bettergradesnowtutoring.com

- Tutor K-12 students in the cities of Moreno Valley, Perris, Riverside, and Corona
- Provide one-on-one tutoring in students' home

ABOUT THE AUTHOR

Dr. David Macauley was born and raised in Freetown, Sierra Leone, West Africa. Upon completing high school, he attended Fourah Bay College, at the University of Sierra Leone, where he graduated with a joint honors bachelor's degree in Zoology and Botany. Dr. Macauley left Freetown in 1991 to continue his education in Southern California.

He was hired by the Los Angeles Unified School District in 1997 and taught Life Science and Biology in middle and high school, respectively. He currently teaches Biology and Earth science at the Moreno Valley Unified school district where he also serves in various leadership positions, including focus group leader for the African American sub-group.

He holds a Master's degree in Multicultural Education and a doctorate in Educational Leadership and Management from California State University at Dominguez Hills, CA, and Capella University in Minneapolis, MN, respectively. Dr. Macauley is also an adjunct professor at the University of California Riverside Extension in Southern California. He instructs students in the teacher-credentialing program.

He is married to his wife, Molley, and together they have two children. Dr. Macauley is an avid chess player and enjoys traveling. His research interests are in motivating African-American male students to increase participation in the Science, Technology, Engineering and Mathematics career pipeline.

ABOUT THE BOOK

Increasing Enrollment of African-American Males in Advanced High School Mathematics and Science Courses, is an action research that highlights barriers that contribute to the disparity and increasing achievement gap between students of color and their counterparts of other ethnicities.

Dr. Macauley provides a framework through which a K-12 institution can objectively examine and address systemic factors that impede the equity and access in the representation of students of color in the STEM pipeline. To counter the plethora of deficit-focused research, he addresses the need for pragmatic solutions through effective teaching that is relevant, high levels of student engagement that is challenging, and support that provides strategic interventions and on-going mentorships.

This book is a must read for parents and those who champion the cause and advocate for maximizing the potential of our students to be adequately prepared to compete on the national and global STEM career opportunities of the 21st Century.

KEY TERMS: academic, accommodations, achievement expectations, achievement gaps, advanced mathematics, advanced placement, advanced science, African-American, Algebra, AP calculus, bias, Big Brothers/Big Sisters Program, classroom practices, collaborative action research, contributing factors, coping skills, counselors, cultural equity, cultural identity, cultural sensitivity, cultural strengths, disadvantaged youths, educational system, ethnic minorities, family communication, global competitiveness, guidance-counseling, honors courses, inductive thematic analysis, Institutional Review Board (IRB), instructional approach, instructional strategies, intervention strategies, language development, male bonding, management principles, marginalized youth, mathematics, mentor-mentee program, mentoring, methodology, parent involvement, pedagogy, pre-calculus, professional growth, racism, remedial courses, Rites of Passage Program (ROP), S.T.E.M. (STEM) Education, school environment, science, self-esteem, social determinants, socio-cultural issues, Sponsor-a Scholar, standardized tests, structured mentoring, student, teacher, tutoring programs

www.ingramcontent.com/pod-product-compliance
Lightning Source LLC
Chambersburg PA
CBHW072003090426
42740CB00011B/2065